Contemporary
COOKING

Volume 3

Contemporary
COOKING

Volume 3

3M

Contemporary Cooking

© Marshall Cavendish Ltd. 1983
© Minnesota Mining & Mfg. Co. 1984

Editorial production by James Charlton Associates, Ltd., New York. Editor-in-Chief, James Charlton; Managing Editors, Barbara Binswanger, Jennie McGregor; Food Editors, Inez M. Krech, Cecile Lamalle, Anne Lanigan, Maria Robbins.

Book production and manufacturing consulting by: Cobb/Dunlop Publishing Services, Inc., New York
Art Direction and interior design by: Marsha Cohen/Parallelogram
Cover design by: Koechel/Peterson Design, Minneapolis

Acknowledgments: Allan Baillie, Pat Cocklin, Delu PAL International, Aire deZanger, Alan Duns, John Elliott, Gus Francisco, Melvin Grey, Gina Harris, Anthony Kay, Paul Kemp, David Levin, David Meldrum, Roger Phillips, Nick Powell, Iain Reid, John Turner, Paul Williams, George Wright, Cuisinarts, Inc.

Printed and bound in Yugoslavia by CGP Delo.

Library of Congress Cataloging in Publication Data
Main entry under title:

Contemporary Cooking.

   Includes index.
   1. Cookery.   I. Minnesota Mining and Manufacturing Company.
TX715.C7586   1984   641.5   84-2563
0-88159-500-4   —   (set)
ISBN: 0-88159-002-9

CONTENTS

for the Contemporary Cooking Series

VOLUME 3

Part One
CLASSIC SAUCES

Sauces have been the subject of a great many debates. There are those who consider them the highest form of the culinary arts. Others maintain that good, plain, honest food is only ruined by all those elaborate sauces. And then there are those who are simply intimidated by them. Sauces often come tagged with foreign names and are associated with very rich, voluptuous meals involving costly and bizarre ingredients such as truffles, larks' tongues and plovers' eggs. A host of otherwise accomplished cooks are still convinced that they can never make a sauce that isn't lumpy or greasy or laced with a burnt and bitter taste. Egg yolks, they feel, will always curdle and mayonnaise will separate and run.

The preparation of sauces should not be intimidating. In fact, the way sauces are made is often much misunderstood. The entire body of French cooking is based primarily on a respect for good ingredients and the enhancement of their natural tastes. Without exception, all the classic sauces are made with wholesome, ordinary foods—juices of meat and poultry that have been boiled or braised; cream, butter, eggs, fresh herbs . . .

A sauce is not intended to overwhelm the food with which it is served. It should complement the flavors and textures of the main ingredient, ideally adding a harmonious balance to the meal. It could be said that a sauce plays an important but supporting role in a meal. Just as in the theater when great actors in supporting parts can make a good production sublime, so can a well-made sauce make good food memorable.

All this is not to say that, looking through the history of what men have eaten, we would not find some quite surprising, and to us disturbing, sauces that were once as popular as bottled ketchup is today.

M. F. K. Fisher provides a recipe from Rome, 400 B.C., for *garum:* "Place in a vessel all the insides of fish, both large fish and small. Salt them well. Expose them to the air until they are completely rotted. Drain off the liquid that comes from them, and it is the sauce garum" *(An*

Alphabet for Gourmets). This was a basic sauce which might be used alone or further enhanced with asafetida, vinegar, dill, mint, dates . . . to be served, perhaps, with chicken.

From Barbara Norman's *Tales of the Table* we learn the following: "A typical fourteenth-century dish is mawmenee. To make this, you take a pottle (two quarts) of sweet wine and two pounds of sugar, clarify sugar with wine, strain it into an earthenware pot, and add cinnamon, cloves, sandalwood for color, and let it cook slowly. When it is neither too thick nor too thin, you add boiled, shredded chicken flesh."

If ever sauces overwhelmed the food, it was in medieval times. Spices, though vastly more expensive than they are now, were much adored and used with great abandon. Sauces, in certain ways, played more important roles in the construction of a meal. Most meat, including poultry, was sinewy and tough, and likely preserved with salt for large parts of the year. Most probably all meat was boiled; even the roasts had to be boiled first to soften them. Meat, for the most part, was served up chopped, shredded, even pounded to a paste. After all the boiling and chopping, one can imagine that some of the flavor was lost. A spicy sauce—mixtures of cloves, cinnamon, vinegar, bread, currants, cardamom, raisins, and lots of verjuice (the sour juice of crab apples or unripe grapes, used much like lemon juice)—supplied the flavor. It is no wonder that Chaucer warned, "Woe to the cook whose sauce has no sting."

Professional sauce makers in Paris sold ready-made concoctions to busy housewives: *green sauce,* made up of herbs, ginger, cloves and cardamom; a pungent *yellow sauce* in which saffron and ginger were the dominant tastes; and the most popular of all, called *cameline sauce,* flavored essentially with cinnamon. All these are a far cry from the foods and sauces that we know today.

By the early eighteenth century a new cuisine was coming about. The reckless use of spices gradually gave way to subtler, simpler preparations. In part this came about as people learned to eat more varied foods. As difficult as it may be for us to comprehend, fresh fruits and vegetables were suspect for a long, long time. With increased variety, the style of cooking took a small but important step towards the philosophy put forth two centuries later by the chef Curnonsky that "Cuisine is when things taste like themselves."

Butter did not come into common use until the seventeenth century. Until that time sauces were thickened with bread, ground nuts, or just raw flour tossed into the pot. The history of sauces took a giant step when someone thought to cook a little flour in some butter, thereby inventing the ultimate in liaisons—the *roux.* It seems like such a simple thing and yet, without it we could not have some of the world's greatest sauces. Without a roux there would not be a béchamel, or velouté, or espagnole, or the greatest of them all, demi-glace.

No one can speak of sauces without acknowledging Marie-Antoine Carême, the greatest chef of nineteenth-century France and still considered to be the founder of classic French cookery. He was unquestionably an artist and a genius. He was ambitious, willful, autocratic. His lifelong goal was nothing less than conquering the world with French cuisine—that is, to have his work recognized as the standard of perfection that all the world aspired to. In many ways his dream came true. He wrote in *Le Cuisinier Parisien* (1828), "Be aware that no foreign sauce is comparable to those of our great modern cuisine. I have been able to experience the difference. I have seen England, Russia, Germany and Italy, and everywhere I have come upon our chefs occupying the top positions in foreign courts." Not the least of his many accomplishments was the orderly system of classification of sauces into the *mother* sauces *(sauces mère)* and the sauces that derive from them.

Few people today would or even could eat the grand and lavish meals Carême created, but his great legacy of sauces is very much alive. The techniques necessary to make the sauces are admirably simple and can be mastered by every cook. Indeed, today nearly every home kitchen is so well equipped that we can reproduce the sauces that were once reserved for royalty. Even the smallest freezer can hold some pints of espagnole (a stock combined with roux, reduced to liquid gold).

With this on hand you have the wherewithal to serve the ultimate in *haute cuisine* in the amount of time it takes to broil a steak.

The other great sauces based on eggs, butter and oil—hollandaise, béarnaise, mayonnaise—so tricky once, have been reduced to child's play by the food processor. No one denies that they are rich. They are indeed and so they are a luxury, a special treat for special times. Great sauces under-line the truth that we would not wish to live by bread alone. We need occasions to remind us that there is luxury and art, that we are civilized and that our taste buds are complex. It would be right to cele-brate the spring—put flowers in our hair, a string of pearls around our neck, and when the first aspar-agus arrives let's serve up hollandaise without re-grets.

WHITE SAUCES

Béchamel and velouté are the basic white sauces. The techniques used in making them are almost identical and they can be prepared quickly. Both are thickened with a *roux*, a mixture of butter and flour cooked slowly over gentle heat. A béchamel, however, is made with milk and a velouté is made with a white stock—poultry, veal or fish.

To Make Roux

Always measure the ingredients before you start cooking. If possible, use a heavy-bottomed saucepan to insure even heat distribution. It should be large enough to hold all the liquid you will be adding to it.

Melt the butter over gentle heat. When the foam has subsided, add the flour. Stir with a wooden spoon to blend flour and butter and cook over gentle heat, stirring constantly. The roux for a white sauce must remain a pale golden straw color—approximately 2 minutes cooking time. While the roux cooks, the butter-flour mixture will froth gently. The cooking eliminates the raw flour taste and swells the

Basic Béchamel Sauce

Makes 1 cup

2   tablespoons unsalted
      butter
2   tablespoons all-purpose
      flour
1   cup milk
      pinch of grated nutmeg
      salt and white pepper

1 Melt butter in a heavy saucepan over low heat.

2 When foam has subsided, stir in flour to make a roux and cook over low heat, stirring constantly, for 2 minutes.

3 Heat milk in a separate saucepan until hot. Do not boil.

4 Off the heat, stir a little of the hot milk into the roux. Gradually stir in the remaining milk until sauce is smooth.

5 Return to medium heat, bring to a boil. Cook 1 minute stirring constantly. Remove from heat, add nutmeg, salt and pepper.

flour's starch particles so the added liquid can be absorbed and thickened. Remove the roux from the heat before adding the hot liquid, but do not allow it to cool. If the roux *has* cooled, reheat it gently before adding the hot liquid.

Béchamel Sauce

The simplest of all white sauces, a basic béchamel takes no longer than 5 minutes to make. Its utter simplicity makes it the perfect sauce for any number of strongly flavored vegetables such as spinach, mushrooms, broccoli and cauliflower. It replaces ricotta in many lasagne recipes and is used in other pasta dishes. It is often called for in dishes that are cooked *au gratin*.

• You will never have a lumpy sauce if your roux is cooked until it bubbles, if the liquid is hot (near the boiling point), and if you beat the liquid in with a wire whisk. Even so, a lumpy sauce can be saved by straining it through a fine-meshed sieve.

• A sauce that is too thin may be boiled down over moderately high heat, but it must be constantly stirred with a wooden spoon so that it does not burn on the bottom and sides.

• A sauce that is too thick may be thinned out by bringing it to a simmer and beating in milk or stock, 1 tablespoon at a time.

A basic béchamel may be flavored with any of these:
• a pinch of cayenne pepper
• a few drops of lemon juice
• a few snips of fresh dill
• a few snips of fresh tarragon

A basic béchamel may be enriched with any of these:
• a few tablespoons of heavy cream
• a tablespoon or two of butter
• a couple of tablespoons of grated Parmesan or Gruyère cheese

Béchamel with Aromatic Vegetables

½ small carrot
½ small onion
½ celery rib
1 cup milk
1 bay leaf

1 Chop vegetables and add to milk. Add bay leaf.

2 Heat milk mixture over low heat to simmering. Remove from heat, cover, and let stand for 30 minutes for flavors to infuse.

3 Strain milk mixture through a sieve into a measuring cup. Discard vegetables. Continue as for a basic béchamel sauce.

Velouté Sauce

A velouté sauce is made in much the same way as a béchamel but because the milk is replaced with stock it produces a more intensely flavored sauce. The stock—chicken, veal or fish—should be chosen according to the food with which the sauce is to be served. It is an excellent sauce to serve with poached chicken, fish, and plainly boiled or steamed vegetables. The creamy stews called *blanquettes* always require a well-made velouté.

The final addition of cream and egg yolks gives a velouté sauce delicacy and richness. These should be added at the very end. The velouté sauce may be made ahead, cooled and refrigerated, or frozen for future use, providing you make the basic sauce only up to the final enrichment.

To reheat the basic sauce it is best to use a double boiler to prevent lumps forming. Place the sauce in the top pan of a double boiler and reheat slowly over hot water, stirring until the mixture is hot. If the sauce becomes at all lumpy, strain it through a fine sieve into a clean pan. When the mixture is hot and smooth, gradually add the egg and cream liaison as described in the basic method.

Velouté Sauce

Makes 1 cup

2   tablespoons unsalted
    butter
2   tablespoons all-purpose
    flour
1   cup hot white stock:
    chicken, veal or fish,
    depending on final dish
1   egg yolk
2   tablespoons thick cream
    salt and white pepper
2   or 3 drops of lemon juice

1 Melt butter in a saucepan over low heat. Stir in the flour to make a roux and cook for about 4 minutes, until it turns a pale beige.

2 Remove from heat. Gradually add hot stock, stirring to keep the mixture smooth.

3 Return to heat. Bring to a boil, stirring constantly. Reduce heat and simmer for 15 minutes.

4 Place egg yolk and cream in a bowl and beat thoroughly to make a liaison.

5 Add 5 tablespoons of the hot velouté sauce to the egg and cream liaison, a little at a time, stirring well.

6 Pour the contents of the bowl into the saucepan in a steady stream, whisking or stirring constantly.

7 Season with salt and pepper to taste and add 2 or 3 drops of lemon juice.

8 Reheat the sauce carefully over low heat, stirring constantly.

Sauces Derived From Béchamel Sauce

Although the basic preparations of béchamel sauce and velouté sauce are excellent on their own and have many uses as such, they are both considered *mother* sauces from which a number of other *daughter* sauces are derived.

Note: All of the following variations are based on 1 cup of *mother* sauce.

Sauce à la Crème

This is a richer version of béchamel; it is used with eggs, vegetables, pasta, fish and poultry.

1 cup béchamel sauce
¼ to ½ cup heavy cream

Heat the béchamel sauce to a simmer and beat in the heavy cream, 1 tablespoon at a time, until the desired consistency is reached.

Sauce Mornay

A classic cheese sauce, most often used to bind or coat vegetables, fish, chicken or eggs that are finished under the broiler with a *gratin* topping.

1 cup béchamel sauce
2 ounces grated Gruyère or other Swiss cheese or equal amounts of grated Gruyère and Parmesan (½ cup)
½ cup heavy cream (optional)
pinch of cayenne pepper (optional)

Heat the béchamel sauce to a simmer and remove from heat. Beat in the cheese, a little at a time, and stir until it has melted and is fully blended with the sauce. If the sauce seems too thick, add the heavy cream, 1 tablespoon at a time. Season with cayenne to taste.

Note: If the Mornay sauce is to be used with fish or chicken, you may wish to substitute stock for the heavy cream.

Sauce Nantua

A delicate and delicately colored sauce, enriched with cream and shellfish. The tails of crayfish are traditionally used, but as they are often unavailable, shrimps make a good substitute. Nantua sauce is excellent with poached fish fillets, poached chicken breasts or hard-cooked eggs.

1 cup béchamel sauce
½ cup heavy cream
2 tablespoons unsalted butter
1 cup peeled uncooked shrimps
sweet paprika (optional)

Combine the béchamel sauce and the heavy cream in a saucepan and simmer for 10 or 15 minutes to reduce the sauce to ½ cup. Melt the butter in a skillet and sauté the shrimps for a few minutes until they turn pink and are just done. Reserve 4 shrimps and process the rest in a blender or food processor to make a fine paste. Off the heat, fold the shrimp paste into the sauce. Add a little paprika for extra color if desired. The sauce should be a pale, rosy color. Fold in reserved whole shrimps.

Sauce Soubise

This is an onion lover's sauce. The sweet, rich flavor of the onions is perfectly set off by the creamy béchamel. It is excellent with simply prepared meat, chicken, turkey, even lamb.

3 tablespoons unsalted butter
5 medium onions, sliced
1 cup thick béchamel sauce (reduce a larger quantity if necessary)
heavy cream or milk, as needed
salt and white pepper
pinch of grated nutmeg

Melt the butter in a large skillet and cook the onions slowly for 20 to 30 minutes, until they are soft but not brown. Watch them carefully and stir often. Heat the béchamel to a simmer and fold in the onions. If sauce is too thick, thin with a few tablespoons of cream or milk. Simmer, uncovered, for 15 minutes, stirring from time to time. Purée through a food mill or in a food processor. Season to taste with salt, pepper and nutmeg.

Sauces Derived From Velouté Sauce

Sauce Allemande

Also known as Sauce Parisienne, it is a basic velouté enriched with egg yolks and heavy cream. It adds a touch of luxury to eggs, fish, poultry and vegetables.

1   cup velouté sauce
2   egg yolks
¼   to ½ cup heavy cream
    salt and white pepper
    lemon juice

Bring the velouté sauce to a simmer. With a wire whisk, beat egg yolks with ¼ cup heavy cream in a mixing bowl. Reserve remaining cream. Beat ½ cup of hot velouté sauce, a few drops at a time, into the egg-yolk and cream mixture, then pour the mixture back into the rest of the sauce. Bring to a boil, stirring constantly, and simmer for 1 minute. Remove from heat and season to taste with salt and pepper and add a few drops of lemon juice. Thin with the reserved cream if sauce is too thick.

Sauce aux Champignons

A mushroom sauce that is an elaboration of the Sauce Allemande. Serve it with veal, chicken or poached fish.

1   cup Sauce Allemande
1   tablespoon butter
4   ounces mushrooms, cleaned and sliced thin
¼   teaspoon salt
    few drops of lemon juice

Heat the Sauce Allemande to a simmer. Melt butter in a skillet, add mushrooms, sprinkle with salt and lemon juice, and sauté briefly until they soften and release their juices. Fold mushrooms into the Sauce Allemande and simmer for 5 minutes.

Sauce Bercy

A justly popular fish sauce to serve with poached fish fillets. After the fish fillets are sauced they may be run under a hot broiler for a minute or two to impart a golden glaze to sauce.

1   cup velouté sauce made with fish stock
2   tablespoons unsalted butter
2   shallots, peeled and minced
1   cup dry white wine
    salt and white pepper
1   tablespoon minced fresh parsley

Heat velouté to a simmer. Melt 1 tablespoon of the butter in a skillet and sauté the shallots until they are soft but not brown. Pour in the wine and boil quickly to reduce by half. Add wine and shallots to the velouté and simmer, stirring, for 1 minute. Season with salt and white pepper to taste. Cut remaining butter into small dice and whisk into the sauce, bit by bit. Remove from heat and add parsley.

Curry Sauce

Although far removed from any traditional Indian curry, this light, piquant sauce is quite delicious nonetheless. Serve it with chicken, turkey, lamb, hard-cooked eggs or any number of vegetables.

1   cup velouté sauce, made with chicken or veal stock
1   cup minced onions
2   tablespoons butter
2   to 3 teaspoons curry powder
    salt and white pepper
    lemon juice
    cayenne pepper (optional)

Heat velouté sauce. Sauté the onions in the butter until soft but not browned. Stir in curry powder and cook, stirring constantly, for a minute or two. Add onion mixture to the velouté and simmer over low heat for 5 to 10 minutes, stirring frequently. Remove from heat and add salt, pepper, lemon juice and cayenne to taste.

Sauce Aurore

A simple, pretty sauce named for the color of a rosy dawn. Serve it with hard-cooked eggs or chicken, quenelles or any delicate fish mousse.

1 cup velouté sauce, made
   with chicken or veal
   stock
3 tablespoons tomato paste
1 tablespoon minced fresh
   basil or tarragon

Heat the velouté and stir in the tomato paste until it is well blended. Garnish with the fresh herb just before serving.

Sauce Chivry

A velouté enlivened with white wine and herbs, a chivry sauce is as delicate and scented as a summer garden. Use with poached chicken breasts, young tender vegetables and eggs.

1 cup dry white wine
4 tablespoons minced fresh
   herbs: tarragon, parsley,
   chervil
2 tablespoons snipped chives
   or the green part of
   scallions
1 shallot, peeled and minced
1 cup velouté sauce, made
   with chicken or veal
   stock
   more minced fresh herbs
   for garnish

Combine the wine, herbs, chives and shallot in a saucepan and bring to a boil. Cook over lively heat until the wine is reduced to 2 or 3 tablespoons. Heat velouté sauce to a simmer and strain the wine and herb infusion through a fine sieve into the velouté. Simmer, stirring occasionally, for another minute or two. Garnish with minced fresh herbs just before serving.

Sauce Normande

The classic sauce to serve with fillets of sole, flounder and other poached fish, but good with mussels and oysters as well.

1 cup velouté sauce made
   with fish stock
1 cup fish stock or poaching
   liquid from fish or clam
   juice
½ cup minced mushrooms
½ cup heavy cream
   white pepper

Combine the velouté, fish stock or other liquid, mushrooms and cream in a heavy saucepan and simmer over medium heat until reduced by half. Strain through a fine sieve, pressing the mushrooms with a wooden spoon to extract all the liquid. Season to taste with pepper.

BROWN SAUCES

Unquestionably, the brown sauces represent one of the highest achievements of French cookery. Although these sauces incorporate a roux or starch-based liaison, they are never thick in the way that the white sauces are. Their consistency is always liquid but with body. Their texture on the tongue is velvety and deep.

The most complex of these, Sauce Espagnole and Demi-Glace Sauce, were developed primarily for the great restaurant kitchens. They are based on long-simmered meat stocks, and represent a large investment in time and ingredients for the home cook. But the procedures involved are not at all difficult and the resulting sauces are glorious indeed. Both these grand sauces are in effect further elaborations and refinements of the easily accomplished Simple Brown Sauce.

Two humbler sauces, the Jus Lié and the Simple Brown Sauce, complete the family of brown sauces. Both these sauces can be prepared quickly and provide, in their simplicity, adaptability and good homemade taste.

All the brown sauces keep very well in the freezer and provide the basis for a number of quickly made and luxurious dinners.

Jus Lié

Makes 1 cup

1   cup beef stock
2   tablespoon cornstarch, or
     1 tablespoon arrowroot

• The mixture of liquid and starch to be used as a liaison is called a *slurry*.
• You may substitute chicken stock, veal stock or even a flavorful vegetable stock to good effect.
• Use minced fresh herbs—parsley, tarragon, dill—for a final garnish.

1 Stir the cornstarch and 2 table-spoons of the cold stock in a medium-size heatproof bowl until smooth.

2 Pour remaining stock into a medium-size saucepan. Heat gently to simmering.

Simple Brown Sauce

Makes 1 cup

1   small carrot
1   small onion
1   tablespoon vegetable oil
1   tablespoon unsalted butter
2   tablespoons all-purpose
     flour
1¾ cups beef stock
     salt
     freshly ground black
       pepper

When making a brown roux:

• Always measure the fat and flour accurately. Fat may exceed flour, but never the other way around.

• The stock should be cold or warm but never hot when added. Remove the pan from the heat before stirring in the stock. Then stir over heat until thickened.

• If the sauce becomes too thick during cooking, it can be thinned with a little stock or water.

1 Wash and chop the carrot. Peel the onion; chop fine.

2 Sauté vegetables in butter and oil until lightly browned.

5 Remove pan from heat and stir in stock in a slow steady stream.

6 Heat sauce to boiling. Reduce heat to bare simmer. Simmer, partially covered, for approximately 45 minutes.

3 Stir cornstarch mixture again. Slowly stir hot stock into cornstarch mixture, stirring constantly until blended.

4 Return stock mixture to saucepan. Heat over medium heat, stirring constantly, to boiling. Boil for 3 minutes.

3 Remove pan from heat and stir in flour until evenly distributed.

4 Cook roux, stirring constantly, until nut brown in color, about 10 minutes.

7 Skim fat and foam from surface of sauce during simmering.

8 Strain sauce through a fine sieve into a clean bowl. Season to taste.

Jus Lié

The least complicated of the brown sauces, a *jus lié,* like velouté, can be produced in minutes. It differs from a velouté in that no roux is used to thicken it. It calls instead for cornstarch or arrowroot dissolved in liquid (a mixture called a slurry) for an extremely light and delicate liaison *(lié).* Its taste depends entirely on a well-flavored stock. Commercial bouillon cubes and canned broths yield unsatisfing results. Homemade stocks, however, and any liquid used to braise a cut of beef, veal or poultry, or juices left over from a stew, should be hoarded away, and used to make *jus lié.*

Brown Roux

A good brown roux, which differs somewhat from the quickly made pale roux used for the béchamel and velouté sauces, is crucial to the success of the other brown sauces.

A brown roux begins with diced aromatic vegetables sautéed in clarified butter or a combination of butter and vegetable oil. When the vegetables begin to brown, flour is stirred in to blend with the vegetables and fat. The roux is cooked over low, even heat and stirred all the while with a wooden spoon until the flour has turned a light brown color. This takes approximately 10 to 15 minutes.

Clarified Butter

Clarified butter can be cooked longer and over higher heat without burning. This is extremely important in making a brown roux because the presence of any burnt particles will give an unpleasant, acrid taste to the entire sauce.

To make clarified butter: Melt 1 pound of unsalted butter in a heavy saucepan. When the butter has turned liquid, skim away the foam that rises to the top, then carefully pour the clear yellow liquid into a bowl. Discard all the milky residue that is left on the bottom. The clear yellow liquid is the clarified butter.

12

This can be done well ahead of time as clarified butter keeps for a long time in the refrigerator.

Simple Brown Sauce

Not quite as simple as a *jus lié,* a simple brown sauce involves less time than the more sophisticated sauce espagnole or demi-glace sauce, and the results can be excellent.

A well-flavored veal or beef stock is added to a brown roux, brought to a boil and simmered over low heat for about 1 hour. During this time the sauce must be regularly skimmed to remove the foam and fat that will rise to the surface. The sauce is then strained and seasoned.

A more richly flavored brown sauce can be achieved by adding a few tablespoons of diced ham to the vegetables in the roux.

Sauce Espagnole

To create Sauce Espagnole, add a *bouquet garni* (fresh parsley, bay leaf, thyme) and fresh tomatoes or tomato paste to the stock; simmer for at least 2 hours, and occasionally skim the fat and froth from the surface. The flavor will be more intense than a simple brown sauce, and the liquid should be thick enough to coat a spoon lightly.

Demi-Glace Sauce

At this point you are but one step removed from the glorious Demi-Glace Sauce. Start with the espagnole, add more brown stock and the *bouquet garni,* and simmer to reduce by half. This will take time because the sauce must simmer on the lowest heat to prevent burning. In addition, it is important to skim frequently. The final sauce will be almost a glaze with viscous texture and a gleaming shiny look.

Storing

All the basic brown sauces keep well, so it is worth making them in large quantities. Any of the four can be stored in a covered jar in the refrigerator for at least a week, but should be brought to the boil again after 4 days. Allow the sauce to cool, then replace it in its covered jar. Brown sauces can also be frozen and stored in the freezer for a month. They should be reheated in exactly the same way as a white sauce.

Sauces Derived From Brown Sauces

As well as being served as sauces on their own, the brown sauces can be the *mother* sauces of a great variety of derivative sauces. The very best sauces are made from sauce espagnole, and the ultimate sauces can only be achieved with a demi-glace mother. In most circumstances, however, admirable results can be achieved with a well-made simple brown sauce as the base.

All the recipes for the following sauces are based on 1 cup of brown sauce; the choice of which sauce is up to you.

Sauce Diable

A peppery sauce that goes well with simply broiled meat and chicken.

2 shallots, peeled and minced
1 tablespoon butter
1 cup dry white wine
1 cup brown sauce
   freshly ground black pepper
   cayenne pepper

Sauté the shallots in butter until they are soft. Add wine and cook over high heat to reduce to about 3 tablespoons. Add the reduction to brown sauce and simmer for 5 minutes. Remove from heat and season with enough black pepper and cayenne to make it spicy.

Sauce Madère

The classic Madeira-flavored sauce to serve with filet of beef, game, chicken livers and ham.

½ cup Madeira wine
1 cup brown sauce
2 tablespoons butter, at room temperature

Heat the wine in a saucepan and boil gently to reduce by half. Add the brown sauce and simmer for 5 minutes. Remove from heat and beat in the butter, a little at a time.

Sauce Duxelles

This is a lively mushroom sauce that goes well with all sorts of chops, broiled or sautéed; chicken, steaks and even pasta.

1 tablespoon butter
1 tablespoon oil
4 ounces mushrooms, minced
3 shallots, peeled and minced
¾ cup dry white wine
1 cup brown sauce
2 tablespoons tomato paste
    salt and black pepper
2 tablespoons chopped fresh parsley

Heat butter and oil in a skillet; when foam subsides add mushrooms and shallots. Cook over medium heat, stirring, until liquid from mushrooms has evaporated and mushrooms have turned dark. Add the wine and boil down to reduce it to about 1 tablespoon. Heat the brown sauce to a simmer and add tomato paste. Stir until well blended, then add the wine reduction, mushrooms and shallots, and simmer for 5 minutes. Remove from heat and taste for seasoning. Add salt and black pepper to taste. Add parsley just before serving.

Sauce Chasseur

A Sauce Duxelles becomes a Sauce Chasseur by adding garlic to the shallots and substituting chopped ripe tomatoes for the tomato paste.

1 tablespoon butter
1 tablespoon oil
4 ounces mushrooms, minced
3 shallots, peeled and minced
1 clove garlic, minced
¾ cup dry white wine
1 cup brown sauce
1 pound ripe tomatoes, peeled, seeded, and chopped
    salt and black pepper
2 tablespoons chopped fresh parsley

Heat butter and oil in a skillet; when foam subsides add mushrooms, shallots and garlic. Cook over medium heat, stirring, until liquid from mushrooms has evaporated and mushrooms have turned dark. Add the wine and boil down to reduce it to about 1 tablespoon. Heat the brown sauce to a simmer and add tomatoes. Stir until well blended, then add the wine reduction, mushrooms and shallots, and simmer for 5 minutes. Remove from heat and taste for seasoning. Add salt and black pepper to taste. Add parsley just before serving.

EMULSION-BASED SAUCES

Warm butter emulsion sauces are a glorious mixture of an acid, such as lemon juice, vinegar or wine, egg yolks and sweet butter. The two most famous of this sauce family are hollandaise and béarnaise. They are classic accompaniments for salmon, grilled steak, lamb, poached fish, asparagus, broccoli and other green vegetables.

Hollandaise Sauce

Pour enough water into the bottom of a double boiler so the top pan clears the water by 2 inches. Heat the water over low heat to a bare simmer. As an alternative, select a bowl that fits snugly into the top of a saucepan, allowing the same clearance.

Place the yolks of 3 large eggs in the top pan of the double boiler and whisk until slightly thickened, about 3 minutes. Remove the top pan from the bottom.

Experienced cooks will use up to 6 tablespoons of unsalted butter per large egg yolk, but 4 tablespoons per yolk will produce a fine sauce with less risk of separation. Our method for making a hollandaise uses part cold butter and part melted, which further reduces the risk.

Gently melt 8 tablespoons of the butter in a small saucepan. Halve the remaining 4 tablespoons of butter and cut each half into small dice. Add half of the diced butter to the yolk mixture, and return the top pan to the bottom of the double boiler. Whisk constantly over the barely simmering water, scraping the bottom and sides, until the mixture is smooth and lightly coats the whisk, and the bottom becomes visible between strokes, about 4 minutes. Remove the top pan again and add remaining diced butter. Whisk until amalgamated, about 1 minute. Slowly whisk in the melted butter, drop by drop. This is the critical moment as the yolks may reject the butter if added too quickly. When half of the melted butter is incorporated and the sauce has the consistency of heavy cream, whisk in the butter in a thin stream. Season with salt and pepper mixed with a little warm lemon juice or water.

If the hollandaise thickens too quickly and becomes lumpy, immediately plunge the insert into a basin or sink of cold water. Allow the sauce to cool for 1 minute, then whisk vigorously to cool the yolks further until they are barely warm. Return top pan of the double boiler to the bottom.

If sauce begins to curdle, remove top pan from the bottom and whisk in 1 or 2 teaspoons cold water. Return to the bottom, making sure the water is barely simmering.

If the sauce separates, transfer it to a clean bowl. Wash the top pan, dry, and add 1 egg yolk. Whisk to blend and very slowly whisk in the separated sauce. Return top pan to the bottom.

If the sauce does not thicken, whisk together 1 teaspoon lemon juice and 1 tablespoon of the thin sauce in a clean bowl. Slowly whisk in the thin sauce and return to the heat.

To lighten too thick a hollandaise, gradually whisk in 1 or 2 tablespoons of hot water.

Blender or Food Processor Hollandaise. Hollandaise can be made very quickly with an electric blender or food processor and is all but foolproof. While it is never quite as silky as a traditional hollandaise, it is a marvelous time saver.

Warm blender jar or processor bowl with hot water; drain and dry. Gently melt butter over low heat. Add yolks to blender jar or processor bowl. Blend at low speed for about 4 seconds. With blade running, add

Hollandaise Sauce

Makes 1 ½ cups

6   ounces unsalted butter
3   large egg yolks
    salt and white pepper
2   tablespoons fresh lemon
    juice

1 Heat water in bottom of double boiler over very low heat to a bare simmer. Bottom of top pan should clear water by 2 inches.

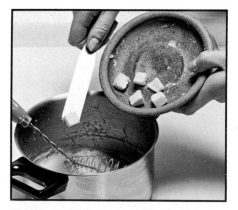

4 Break egg yolks into a small bowl. (Reserve whites for other uses.)

5 Whisk yolks in top of double boiler off heat until creamy and pale yellow, about 2 minutes.

8 Add the remaining diced butter off the heat. Whisk until the butter is amalgamated, approximately 1 minute.

9 Whisk in melted butter, off the heat, making sure each addition is thoroughly incorporated.

melted butter in a thin, steady stream. Continue to blend until sauce is thick and smooth. Season to taste with salt and pepper, add lemon juice, and blend for an additional 4 seconds.

Béarnaise Sauce

Béarnaise is a thicker and stronger flavored cousin of hollandaise. To make, combine wine, vinegar, shallots and tarragon in a saucepan. Boil over high heat until reduced to 2 tablespoons. Strain the wine-vinegar reduction before adding to egg yolks, and proceed as with a hollandaise sauce.

Makes 1½ cups

- ¼ cup dry white wine
- ¼ cup white-wine vinegar
- 2 shallots, peeled and minced
- 1 tablespoon minced fresh tarragon, or ½ tablespoon dried
- 3 large egg yolks
- 6 ounces unsalted butter
- salt and white pepper

Blender or Food Processor Béarnaise. To make béarnaise in a blender or food processor, melt the butter and let cool. Place egg yolks in blender jar or processor bowl and blend while adding wine-vinegar reduction. Continue blending while dribbling in the melted butter until mixture is thick and smooth. Season to taste.

Mayonnaise

Mayonnaise, the "mother" of cold emulsion sauces, is made from uncooked egg yolks that are coaxed into absorbing oil and then holding it in suspension.

To start, all ingredients, as well as a bowl and whisk, must be at room temperature.

Place the bowl, large enough to accommodate the mayonnaise and a balloon whisk, on a damp kitchen towel to anchor it. Place 2 yolks from large fresh eggs in the bowl (1 yolk will

2 Cut 4 tablespoons of the butter in half and cut each half into small dice. Set aside in cool place.

3 Gently melt remaining butter in small saucepan over low heat. Pour into measuring cup and set aside in warm place.

6 Add half of the diced butter to yolk mixture and place over barely simmering water.

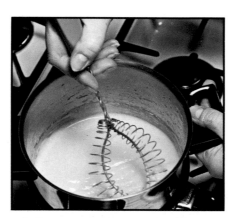

7 Whisk egg-yolk mixture, scraping bottom and sides, until it lightly coats whisk and bottom of pan is visible between strokes.

10 When half of melted butter is absorbed, whisk in remainder in thin steady stream.

11 When all the butter in incorporated and the sauce is thick, season with salt and pepper. Stir in lemon juice.

Mayonnaise

Makes 1½ cups

2   large egg yolks, at room temperature
1   tablespoon—white wine vinegar or fresh lemon juice
½   teaspoon dry mustard
½   teaspoon salt
1   cup olive oil, or peanut oil, vegetable oil or a blend, at room temperature

Mayonnaise can be flavored in various ways. Add:

• 1 tablespoon minced fresh herbs

• 1 garlic clove, crushed or put through a press

• 1 tablespoon curry paste

All olive oil makes for a very strong taste, while peanut or vegetable oil or a blend makes for a lighter and less costly mayonnaise.

1 Whisk room temperature egg yolks in large bowl until pale yellow and sticky, about 2 minutes.

2 Add vinegar or lemon juice, mustard and salt. Whisk until thoroughly combined.

3 Add oil, 1 drop at a time, to yolks.

4 Whisk well after each drop of oil, making sure to scrape bottom and sides of bowl.

5 When mixture thickens and one third of the oil is incorporated, begin adding oil in a thin steady stream, whisking constantly.

6 If mixture becomes too thick, beat in water, lemon juice or vinegar, a few drops at a time until it has the proper consistency.

7 Mayonnaise should have the texture of softly whipped cream and hold its shape, dropping from the whisk with a soft plop.

absorb up to ⅔ cup oil), and whisk until smooth, thick and sticky, 1 to 2 minutes. Blend in the seasonings, about ½ teaspoon each of prepared mustard, salt, and a little freshly ground white pepper if you wish. A tablespoon of fresh lemon juice or wine vinegar will add flavor and encourage the yolks to receive and retain the oil.

Pour the measured oil into a measuring cup or bottle fitted with a cork with 2 V-shaped notches opposite each other. The oil will slowly dribble out one notch while air enters the other.

Add the oil to the yolks slowly at first, drop by drop, whisking continually to incorporate each drop. When the mixture becomes a thick yellow paste and about one third of the oil has been incorporated, add the oil in a thin steady stream, whisking constantly. When finished, the mayonnaise should hold its shape and fall from the whisk with a plop. Whisk 1 or 2 tablespoons boiling water, mixed with any additional seasonings, into the mayonnaise to stabilize it further.

To lighten overly thick mayonnaise, stir in a little lemon juice, vinegar or water.

If the mayonnaise begins to curdle or separate in the initial stages, vigorously whisk in a few drops of cold water. To salvage a completely curdled mayonnaise, whisk an egg yolk in a clean bowl. Slowly whisk in the broken mixture, stopping frequently to make sure it is being reincorporated. Add a little extra lemon juice, vinegar or water since this mayonnaise will be thicker with the additional egg yolk.

Blender or Food Processor Mayonnaise. Use whole eggs (1 whole egg to 1 scant cup of oil) since the blender will not effectively blend just yolks. Place the whole eggs and the seasonings in the blender jar or processor bowl. Cover and blend for about 4 seconds. Then, with the blender running, pour in the oil in a thin steady stream. Blend for an additional 10 seconds.

Halibut Mayonnaise

	4 portions
4	halibut steaks, 6 ounces each (see note)
	salt and white pepper
½	lemon
4	ounces black grapes

2	seedless oranges
2	tablespoons light cream
1	cup homemade Mayonnaise (see facing page)
	watercress sprigs
	crisp lettuce leaves

Cook the halibut for this dish only a few hours before you plan to serve it to retain its delicate taste and texture.

Note: See Part Two for cooking instructions.

Halibut Mayonnaise (continued)

1 Lightly oil a large piece of aluminum foil and place the halibut steaks on it.

2 Sprinkle salt and white pepper over the fish. Squeeze the lemon and pour juice over the fish.

3 Wrap the foil around the fish to make a secure parcel and refrigerate until ready to be cooked.

4 Set the parcel in a steamer and steam the fish for 15 to 20 minutes. Remove from the steamer and open to cool the fish.

5 Halve the grapes and remove the seeds. Peel the oranges completely and cut them into thin slices.

6 Using a spatula, transfer the steaks to a wire rack over a dish. Remove the center bones and the skin.

7 Stir the cream into the mayonnaise and coat each steak with a thick layer of the mayonnaise.

8 Decorate the coated steaks with the prepared grape halves and a sprig of watercress.

9 Line a dish with washed and dried lettuce leaves. Arrange fish on it and garnish with the orange slices.

Curried Chicken Salad

6 portions

2 pounds whole chicken breasts from frying chickens	1 ¼ cups Mayonnaise (see Index)
½ teaspoon salt	1 tablespoon curry paste (see note)
1 large bay leaf	3 tablespoons chopped mango chutney
1 celery rib with leaves	4 tablespoons minced mixed chervil, parsley and chives
1 small onion, peeled	
1 head of Bibb lettuce	
½ head of Boston lettuce	

Rinse chicken pieces; do not remove skin or bones; these add flavor. Split the whole breasts into halves. Put them in a heavy saucepan and add the salt, bay leaf, celery and whole peeled onion. Add enough water just to cover the chicken pieces, and bring it to a boil. Immediately reduce to a simmer and cook for 10 minutes. Test with a skewer; the meat should be tender but still juicy, just slightly underdone. If not done to your taste, cook for a few minutes longer. Cool the chicken in the liquid; it will be completely done when cool.

Remove chicken from the liquid; peel off skin and remove bones. (Skin and bones can be returned to the pan and the liquid can be cooked to make a thin stock.) Reserve the liquid. Cut the chicken into portions; each breast half should make about 4 pieces.

Wash and dry the lettuces, tear or cut into pieces, and arrange around the edge of a round serving platter. Spoon

mayonnaise into a large bowl and stir in the curry paste until completely blended. Fold in the chutney and minced herbs. If the mayonnaise is very thick and stiff, stir in some of the reserved cooking liquid, 1 tablespoon at a time, until it reaches the desired consistency. Add the chicken pieces to the dressing and gently mix until all the pieces have a light coating of the dressing. Arrange the chicken in the center of the platter. Serve cold.

Note: Curry paste is available wherever spices are sold. If you cannot find it, mix 2 teaspoons curry powder with 4 table-spoons white-wine vinegar in a small pan and cook over hot water until the curry powder is completely dissolved and the starches in the curry spices are cooked. Let cool, then stir into the mayonnaise.

Tournedos Henri IV

4 portions

4 large freshly cooked artichoke bottoms (see note)
6 ounces large mushrooms
4 thick slices of firm bread
6 tablespoons clarified butter (see index)

4 beef tournedos, each 4 ounces
salt and pepper
1 cup Béarnaise Sauce (see Index)
watercress sprigs

Trim artichoke bottoms to make smooth cups. Wipe mushrooms with a damp cloth, trim base of stems, and cut mushrooms into halves or thick slices. Use a pastry cutter to cut out a large round from each slice of bread.

Heat 4 tablespoons of the butter in a skillet and sauté the bread rounds until golden brown on both sides. Remove these toasts from the skillet to a baking sheet and keep them warm in a low oven. Melt remaining butter in the skillet and sauté the mushrooms over brisk heat until lightly browned; stop cooking before mushrooms lose their juices. With a slotted spoon transfer mushrooms to a metal bowl and keep them warm in the oven.

Tie the tournedos with string to keep them round. Brush them on both sides with the butter remaining in the skillet and broil in a preheated broiler 5 inches from the heat source for 3 minutes on each side for rare. Meanwhile reheat the artichoke bottoms in simmering water for a few minutes.

Place the toasted rounds on a warmed serving platter. Place a tournedos on each round and a well-drained and dried artichoke bottom on each tournedos. Spoon béarnaise sauce into each artichoke, as much as it will hold (usually 4 to 5 teaspoons). Arrange the mushrooms around the steaks and add watercress sprigs. Serve at once.

Traditionally these tournedos are accompanied by sautéed new potatoes, cooked in clarified butter until tender, about 30 minutes. They are turned often and sprinkled with salt toward the end of cooking. For 4 portions, prepare 12 small potatoes.

Note: Canned artichoke bottoms can be substituted when fresh are not available.

Mushroom Velouté

1¼ cups

- 2 ounces fresh mushrooms
- 2 tablespoons unsalted butter
- 3 tablespoons all-purpose flour
- 1 cup chicken stock, hot

- 1 raw egg yolk
- 2 tablespoons heavy cream
  salt and white pepper
- 3 drops of fresh lemon juice

Wipe mushrooms with a damp cloth and trim the base of the stems. Do not peel the mushrooms, but chop caps and stems to very small pieces. Melt the butter in a saucepan over low heat. Remove from heat and stir in the flour. Return pan to low heat and cook and stir the roux until it turns pale beige, about 4 minutes. Remove pan again from heat and pour in the hot stock, stirring all the while to keep the mixture smooth. Add chopped mushrooms. Return saucepan to heat and bring to a boil, stirring constantly. Reduce heat, cover, and simmer for 15 minutes. Strain the sauce through a fine sieve into a clean saucepan, pressing hard to get all the juices from the mushrooms.

In a small bowl, beat egg yolk and cream thoroughly to make a liaison. Gradually add 5 tablespoons of the hot sauce, stirring well. Pour the mixture into the rest of the sauce in a steady stream, whisking constantly. Season with salt and white pepper to taste and add the lemon juice. Keep sauce warm over hot water until ready to serve.

New Potatoes with Mushroom Velouté

4 portions

- 16 small new potatoes
- 6 ounces fresh mushrooms
  salt
- 1¼ cups Mushroom Velouté (preceding recipe)

  chopped parsley and
  grated lemon rind
  (optional)

Wash potatoes. Put them in a saucepan and cover with boiling water. Simmer for 18 to 20 minutes after the water returns to the boil. Drain. When cool enough to handle, carefully peel them. Place in a metal bowl and keep warm over hot water or in a low oven.

Wipe mushrooms with a damp cloth and trim the base of the stems. Cut into slices through cap and stem. Put in a saucepan with a pinch of salt and cover with cold water. Bring to a boil and simmer for 2 minutes. Use a skimmer to lift mushrooms from the blanching liquid and add them to the potatoes.

Prepare the sauce. Turn potatoes and mushrooms into a serving dish and pour the sauce over them. If you like, garnish with parsley and grated lemon rind.

Cheese Sauce with Mustard

3 cups

- 4 tablespoons unsalted butter
- 4 tablespoons all-purpose flour
- 2 cups milk

  salt and white pepper
- 1 teaspoon dry mustard
- 4 ounces Cheddar cheese, shredded (1 cup)

Melt the butter in a heavy saucepan over low heat. Add flour and stir for 2 minutes. Remove saucepan from heat. Heat the milk until very warm and gradually stir it into the roux. Season with salt and white pepper to taste. Return saucepan to heat and stir constantly until sauce comes to a boil. Cover and simmer for 15 minutes, stirring occasionally. Remove saucepan from heat and stir in the mustard and the shredded cheese. The cheese will melt in the retained heat of the sauce. Do not heat after cheese is added, or cheese will become stringy.

Ham and Leeks au Gratin

4 portions

8 medium-size leeks
2 slices of 2-day-old whole-wheat bread
8 thin slices of cooked ham

1½ to 2 cups Cheese Sauce with Mustard (preceding recipe)
4 tablespoons unsalted butter

Wash leeks carefully; cut off roots but keep the base intact so leeks do not fall apart; trim the green leaves to make all the leeks about 6 inches long, or the same size as the length of the ham slices. Bring 1 inch of water to a boil in a large pot. Add leeks and steam for 12 to 15 minutes, until they are tender when tested with a thin skewer. Lift leeks from the water and drain; discard the water.

Preheat oven to 400°F. Remove crusts from bread slices and make crumbs in a blender or food processor, or use a hand grater. Wrap each leek in a slice of ham; place the rolls, seam side down, in a shallow ovenproof dish. Pour cheese sauce over the rolls, using as much as you need to cover the rolls well. Sprinkle bread crumbs evenly on top. Cut the butter into tiny bits and dot them over the crumbs. Bake in the oven until the ham rolls are hot and the top browned and crisp.

Sauce Nivernaise

1¼ cups

2 shallots
1 garlic clove
5 leaves of fresh tarragon
3 tablespoons dry white wine
2 tablespoons tarragon vinegar

1 teaspoon minced fresh parsley
4 ounces unsalted butter, cold
2 egg yolks
salt and white pepper
2 teaspoons fresh lemon juice

Peel and mince shallots. Peel garlic and put through a press into a glass custard dish; set aside. Wash and dry tarragon leaves and snip with scissors to very small bits. Pour wine and vinegar into a small non-aluminum saucepan. Add shallots and snipped tarragon and boil over high heat until reduced to 2 tablespoons of liquids and solids. Strain the infusion and set aside to cool.

Work the garlic and parsley into 2 tablespoons of the butter and shape into a smooth pat. Cut the butter pat into small dice and set aside. Melt remaining butter in a saucepan over low heat. In the top pan of a double boiler, whisk the egg yolks until light and fluffy. Add the strained wine and vinegar reduction and whisk into the eggs for ½ minute. Set the top pan over simmering water in the lower pan.

Add half of the diced butter to the egg-yolk mixture and whisk the sauce for 2 minutes, scraping the sides and bottom of the pan. When the mixture becomes thick, remove the pan from heat and gradually whisk in the rest of the diced butter.

Now pour in half of the melted butter, drop by drop, whisking after each addition until incorporated and the sauce has the consistency of heavy cream. Add the rest in a thin stream, still whisking all the while. Season with salt and white pepper to taste. Stir in the lemon juice. Keep the sauce warm over hot water.

Shredded Fennel with Sauce Nivernaise

4 portions

2 large fennel bulbs
½ teaspoon salt
1 small bay leaf

2 peppercorns, crushed
1¼ cups Sauce Nivernaise (preceding recipe)

Wash fennel; remove coarse outer ribs, the whole upper part of the ribs, and trim the base. Chop or snip enough of the feathery green leaves to make 4 tablespoons and set aside for garnish. Shred the tender fennel hearts from top to bottom and drop into a large saucepan. Add salt, bay leaf and peppercorns, and pour in enough water to cover the shreds. Bring to a boil and simmer for 10 to 12 minutes; do not overcook the fennel or it will be mushy. Drain fennel, rinse with cold water, and drain again. Return to the saucepan and steam for a minute to reheat it.

Pour the sauce nivernaise over the fennel and toss gently. Transfer to a serving bowl and garnish the top with the reserved fennel leaves.

Variations: This recipe is also excellent for other vegetables, especially artichokes, leeks and Jerusalem artichokes.

Beurre Blanc or Beurre Nantais

(White Butter from Nantes)

1 cup

2 shallots	¼ cup white-wine vinegar
8 ounces unsalted butter	1 tablespoon minced fresh
½ cup dry white wine	parsley

Peel and mince the shallots. Let the butter soften at room temperature. Boil the wine, vinegar and shallots in a non-aluminum saucepan until reduced to about 1 tablespoon of liquids and solids. Remove saucepan from heat and beat in the softened butter, 1 tablespoon at a time. The butter should not melt but should be emulsified into the infusion. Add chopped parsley and continue beating until sauce is light and fluffy, and the butter is white. Keep *beurre blanc* warm, not hot, in the top pan of a double boiler over warm water. This sauce can also be frozen. Serve with fish and shellfish.

Sole with Beurre Blanc and Fried Parsley

4 portions

⅓ cup all-purpose flour	½ cup clarified unsalted
½ teaspoon salt	butter
¼ teaspoon freshly ground white pepper	8 to 12 fresh parsley sprigs
4 fillets of sole or other flat fish, 2 pounds altogether	2 cups vegetable oil
	1 cup Beurre Blanc (preceding recipe)

Combine flour, salt and pepper. Rinse the fillets and pat dry. Sole fillets may weigh about 8 ounces; smaller flounders will weigh only 4 ounces. If you are using flounders, purchase 2 fillets for each portion. Dip fillets on both sides into the seasoned flour. Heat clarified butter in a large sauté pan. Add fillets in a single layer and sauté on both sides, allowing 2 minutes a side. If the fillets are thick, you may need to allow an extra minute on each side.

Meanwhile, wash and dry parsley sprigs; remove most of the stems, leaving only enough to serve as a handle. Heat the oil in a frying pan or in a wok to 400°F. Add parsley sprigs, a few at a time, and fry for about 1 minute. Use a slotted spoon to lift parsley from the oil to paper towels to drain. Parsley should be crisp and dark green.

Transfer the cooked fillets to a warmed serving dish. Spoon a dollop of *beurre blanc* on each fillet and garnish with fried parsley. Serve at once.

Poulet Sauté Chasseur

(Chicken with Tomato and Mushroom Sauce)

6 portions

1	chicken, 4 pounds, cut into serving pieces	2	tablespoons vegetable oil
1	teaspoon salt	4	ounces button mushrooms
½	teaspoon white pepper	1¼	cups Chasseur Sauce (see Index)
4	tablespoons unsalted butter		

Rinse chicken pieces and pat dry. Rub salt and pepper over chicken. Melt the butter with the oil in a large flameproof casserole over medium heat. Add chicken pieces in a single layer and sauté, turning pieces frequently, for 8 to 10 minutes, until all are evenly browned. If the pan does not hold all in a single layer, brown them in batches, using part of the butter and oil for each batch.

Wipe the mushrooms with a damp cloth and trim the base of the stems. Add mushrooms to the chicken, cover the casserole, and cook over low heat for 20 to 25 minutes, until chicken is tender.

Transfer chicken to a warmed serving platter. With a slotted spoon lift out the mushrooms and arrange around the platter. Spoon chasseur sauce over the chicken, or serve separately in a warmed sauceboat. To give the chicken additional flavor, pour the sauce into the casserole 10 minutes before the chicken is done and finish cooking in the sauce.

Horseradish Sauce, Cold

1½ cups

1	teaspoon lemon juice	¼	teaspoon white pepper
2	teaspoons vinegar	1	teaspoon sugar
1	teaspoon prepared mustard	3	tablespoons grated fresh horseradish
½	teaspoon salt	¾	cup heavy cream

In a medium-size mixing bowl combine lemon juice, vinegar, mustard, salt, white pepper and sugar. Stir until mustard, salt and sugar are completely dissolved. Stir in the grated horseradish. Whip the cream until almost stiff; do not overbeat it, for it will stiffen further as it is mixed into the cold ingredients. Gently fold the cream into the horseradish mixture, and spoon into a serving bowl, heaping it up in the center. Serve cold with hot roast beef or cold beef dishes.

Horseradish Sauce, Hot

1½ cups

1¼	cups Béchamel Sauce (see Index)	¼	teaspoon white pepper
2	tablespoons grated fresh horseradish	½	teaspoon prepared mustard
½	teaspoon salt	1	teaspoon vinegar
		½	teaspoon sugar

Pour the béchamel sauce into a medium-size saucepan and stir in the rest of the ingredients. Warm over moderate heat, stirring constantly, until sauce is heated through. Pour sauce into a warmed sauceboat and serve hot with roast beef, boiled beef or corned beef.

Shrimp Cocktail with Tomato-Flavored Mayonnaise

4 portions

1 head of Boston lettuce
12 ounces cooked shrimps in shells, at least 24

1 cup Tomato-Flavored Mayonnaise (following recipe)
paprika
4 lemon wedges

Separate the lettuce into leaves: wash and dry leaves. Separate the inner small leaves and shred them. Store whole leaves and shredded leaves separately. Set aside 8 shrimps for garnish and leave them unpeeled. Peel the rest, devein them, and gently fold them into the mayonnaise. (If shrimps are very large, you may wish to split them lengthwise for easier serving.)

Line 4 wineglasses with the whole lettuce leaves, then make a bed in each with the shredded lettuce. Divide shrimps and sauce among the glasses. Sprinkle some paprika on the top. Garnish each portion with a lemon wedge and 2 unpeeled shrimps, arranged on the edge of the glass.

Tomato-Flavored Mayonnaise

1 cup

1 large egg yolk	few drops of
¼ teaspoon dry mustard	Worcestershire sauce
⅛ teaspoon salt	dash of Tabasco®
1 tablespoon lemon juice or	3 tablespoons tomato purée
vinegar	lemon juice
¼ cup corn oil	white pepper
¼ cup olive oil	

Bring all the ingredients to room temperature. Warm the mixing bowl by immersing it in hot water; drain and dry well. Beat the egg yolk in the bowl for 2 minutes before adding the mustard, salt and 1 tablespoon lemon juice or vinegar; beat again. Beat in the oil, both kinds mixed or one kind at a time, drop by drop, until about half is added and the emulsion is thick and creamy. Rest the oil container on the edge of the bowl and trickle in the rest of the oil, beating all the time.

When the mayonnaise is completed, fold in the Worcestershire, Tabasco and tomato purée. Add extra lemon juice, salt and white pepper to taste. Refrigerate, and use within 2 days.

Cauliflower au Gratin

4 to 6 portions

1 large head cauliflower	4 ounces Cheddar cheese
2 cups Cheese Sauce	grated (1 cup)
with Mustard	
(see index)	

Steam a large head of cauliflower until tender but still crisp. Drain and place in a flameproof pan, either the whole head, or the head cut into flowerets. Spoon 2 cups of cheese sauce with mustard over the cauliflower and sprinkle with 1 cup grated Cheddar cheese. Broil in a preheated broiler until the top is bubbly and lightly browned.

Aïoli

(Garlic Mayonnaise)

1 cup

2 garlic cloves	¼ teaspoon salt
1 egg yolk, at room	½ cup olive oil
temperature	

Peel garlic. Beat the egg yolk in a warmed bowl for 2 minutes. Put garlic through a press into the egg and add the salt. Beat the mixture again. Drop by drop, beat in half of the oil; the aïoli will begin to thicken and become creamy. Trickle in the rest of the oil, beating constantly. Cover tightly and refrigerate for up to 2 hours. Be sure to use the day it is made. Serve with fish, shellfish, vegetables.

Note: This recipe can easily be doubled, and the proportions can be altered; more garlic can be used, and 3 egg yolks for 1 cup of oil. If the completed aïoli is very thick and stiff, it can be thinned by adding boiling water, 4 teaspoons for this amount; add 1 teaspoon at a time.

Provençal Vegetable Salad with Aïoli

4 portions

8	new potatoes
6	young carrots
4	ounces green snap beans
1½	cups shelled fresh or frozen lima beans

1½	cups shelled fresh or frozen green peas
1	cup Aïoli (preceding recipe)
	lettuce leaves, garden lettuce or romaine

Scrub and quarter the potatoes and carrots. (If you prefer, both can be scraped or peeled.) Wash green beans and top and tail them. Place potatoes in a large steamer and steam for 10 minutes. Add carrots, lima beans and peas; steam for 5 minutes longer. Add green snap beans and steam for another 5 minutes, until all the vegetables are tender. Remove from the steamer, drain, rinse with very cold water, and drain well.

Chop carrots, potatoes and green beans to the size of the lima beans. Put all the vegetables in a bowl and spoon *aïoli* over them; toss gently to coat the vegetables with the sauce. Spoon the salad onto lettuce leaves on a large serving platter or on individual salad plates. For a party, the salad may be placed in a shallow bowl and unmolded so that it retains the bowl shape. Decorate with strips of pimento. Serve as a salad or as a first course.

Part Two

STEAMING AND POACHING FISH AND POULTRY

The man or woman who discovered that something tasted better after being thrown in the fire was a technological pioneer of sorts, but it was the discovery of how to put something inside something else before bringing it anywhere near the fire that opened up most of the technical controls over the cooking process as we know it. Spit-roasting and broiling were followed at a distance of many millennia by some form of steaming and poaching; cooking, that is, by the action (respectively) of live steam or hot liquid. It was these that first made possible a really significant degree of refinement and subtlety in controlling the effects of heat on food. They remain the most delicate of cooking methods and among the best suited for delicate foods—fish and much other seafood, as well as chicken and the great majority of vegetables.

In one approach to the steaming method, the food is tightly enclosed in some other material so that it will cook in its own sealed-in steam as the internal juices reach boiling temperature. Probably the first material used as a sealant was mud. A surviving example of this very ancient technique is the popular Chinese dish "beggar's chicken." It should be observed that when earthenware pots superseded fresh mud, the change did not automatically mean an abandonment of the steaming principle, for even today there are kinds of unglazed earthenware that are prepared for the oven by soaking them in water so that the food will cook in the steam that they release.

The old custom of sealing food in a heavy crust of moistened salt (sometimes mixed with flour) that is broken open after cooking can also be traced back to the prehistoric mud method. Husks and leaves fulfill the same purpose in many cuisines; the cornhusks used for tamales or the banana leaves in which foods are wrapped in some tropical cuisines are precisely equivalent to the parchment used for fish *en papillote* or the aluminum foil in which we seal some oven-heated foods to cook them in their own steam.

Cooking food in hot water—which is basically what poaching is—requires a sturdy vessel that will hold water, and though objects like tortoise shells and hollow gourds have been pressed into service for this purpose by primitive peoples, the technique as we know it had to await the development of fireproof kettles.

In modern usage, poaching—the name is thought to derive from the French word for pouch or pocket *(poche),* referring to the envelope of white that forms around a poached egg—is often defined in fairly narrow terms. Strictly speaking, it should apply to all cookery in which food is placed directly in a pot of liquid. However, many cooks deplore the idea of letting the concept of poaching verge at any point on that of boiling and insist that properly poached foods must never cook at anything above a gentle simmer because the violence of boiling water tends to toughen some foods and disintegrate others.

There remains to be mentioned yet another form of steaming that came, like poaching, with the development of fireproof pots: the variant in which the food sits on a rack or platform above boiling water, being directly exposed to rising steam and water vapor. This method is of fairly recent standing in most Western cuisines except as applied to steamed puddings (for example, Boston brown bread) and a few other special dishes. However, the method has long been known in the Orient, and has now come into favor in this country for its usefulness in preserving the nutrients and original flavors of foods. Today it is considered the nutritionally soundest way of preparing most fresh vegetables, and it is eminently suited to most seafood as well.

The great advantage of both poaching and steaming is that the food is simultaneously heated and insulated from excessive heat. Fire-roasting or cooking in oil can involve searingly hot temperatures; with poaching and steaming the boiling point of water, 212°F, forms a built-in limitation.

While the hot water or steam cooks the food, it also cushions it against the real heat of the stove. These methods are therefore excellent for fragile-textured foods like fish that require merely to be heated through and are damaged by prolonged exposure to high temperatures.

Nothing more plainly bespeaks elegance than a poached whole fish. Hot or cold, it is one of the classics of most cuisines that have ample access to fish. The fish is usually poached in water or a court bouillon, often with a little white wine and a few aromatic herbs and vegetables. In most cases only enough liquid is used to moisten (rather than submerge) the fish. But in cooking *au bleu*—a method particularly good for freshwater fish, especially trout—the fish is plunged into a generous amount of boiling water or court bouillon well acidulated with vinegar, which turns the skin a striking blue color. Sauces for poached fish—indeed for most poached foods—tend to be rich and full-bodied. Most seafood is lean to begin with, and poaching underscores its leanness; even the fattier fish are light-textured enough to make some contrasting richness extremely pleasant. Hot fish is delicious with butter-based emulsions like hollandaise or *beurre blanc;* cold fish does well with a good mayonnaise or served *chaudfroid* (masked in a velouté stiffened with aspic and enriched with cream and egg yolks). Sauce or no sauce, poaching is a method that demands the best intrinsic quality in the food to be poached; it uncompromisingly exposes real flavor or lack of flavor, and will not flatter less-than-perfect fish or shellfish.

Because of their shape, fish present problems in the selection of a suitable pot, since they do not fit in the usual saucepan or kettle. A long narrow vessel called a *poissonnière* or fish poacher has been devised to solve the problem. There is even a poacher of irregular diamond shape called a *turbotière* (turbot poacher), specially made to accommodate the odd contours of that esteemed North Atlantic flatfish. Fish poachers usually have an inset with handles on which the fish can be lifted out whole after cooking.

Chicken, the chief kind of poultry prepared by

poaching, is endlessly versatile when handled by this method. Poaching produces a fine broth that can then serve as the basis of a sauce, and also ensures that the breast meat will still be moist when the leg joints are done. The repertory of classic chicken dishes extends from the basic *poule-au-pot* (a poached stuffed chicken served with its own broth and the soup vegetables) to rich *chaudfroid* presentations or the sumptuous *poularde en demi-deuil* (chicken in half-mourning), in which thin slivers of black truffle are liberally inserted under the skin.

Boned minced poultry can also be stuffed back into the skin and poached to make a galantine; this is one of the most elegant ways in which duck and goose are poached. Minced mixtures are also poached in the shape of small balls or dumplings in many cuisines; various sorts of poached meatballs, fish balls, and liver or marrow dumplings are to be found under various names throughout most of Eastern Europe. The most celebrated are the gefilte fish of the Eastern European Jews (which originated as a fish galantine, the mixture being sewn back into the skin for poaching) and the quenelles of the French.

Quenelles are the object of much awe and trepidation on the part of beginning cooks, but they are really nothing more or less than very light and smooth-textured dumplings based on a force-meat mixture called a *mousseline* (literally, muslin), containing meat, poultry or fish minced and pounded extremely smooth, beaten eggs or (more often) egg whites, and heavy cream. Sometimes quenelles are also fortified with a starch base, or *panade,* of moistened bread crumbs or *pâte à choux,* folded into the basic mousseline.

Any kind of fish or shellfish can be used, but for the lighter, less starchy quenelles freshwater fish is often preferred because its gelatinous texture helps the little dumplings hold together. Pike is generally agreed to be the finest fish for quenelles. Chicken quenelles, a favorite nonfish variant, also have the advantage of considerable natural gelatin in the meat itself.

Though poaching is as well-recognized a technique in China as in the West, many of the foods we tend to poach are steamed there in the ingenious Chinese bamboo steamer baskets, made to sit above a wok or other pot of boiling water. The most magnificent of these presentations is a steamed whole fish, as expressive of simple luxury as a French-style poached whole fish. The fish, set on a plate in the steamer basket, is anointed with a few simple flavorings (finely shredded gingerroot and scallions figure in a favorite version) and served after cooking either with a pungent dipping sauce or, more simply, with the juices that have collected on the plate in cooking.

The Chinese have also developed a particularly savory way of steaming chicken in a special vessel known as a Yunnan pot, an efficient clay device that has, instead of a flat bottom, a central spout to admit steam from the pan of water over which the covered pot is placed. The chicken, cut into small pieces, is steamed until tender with gingerroot and scallions, then served with the cooking liquid much after the manner of a steamed fish or a *pot-au-feu.*

All of these dishes require the simplest of handling and the best of ingredients; indeed, they reveal the subtlety and refinement that ought to be the *raison d'être* of basic moist-heat cookery.

STEAMING AND POACHING

Steaming and poaching are two moist-heat cooking methods especially well suited to fish, shellfish and poultry. In steaming, the food is cooked only by steam arising from the liquid used; in poaching the food is covered with liquid, usually flavored in some way, and cooked at a temperature below boiling, 190° to 200°F, no hotter. The water must never boil because the higher heat of boiling causes the fibers of the food to shrink and juices to escape into the liquid; while that would enrich the poaching liquid, as in making stock, it would result in a dry and tasteless food.

Steaming is a very quick method if the food is properly chosen and prepared. Also, it preserves flavor and nutrients because the relatively low temperature of the food as it cooks prevents escape of the nutrients. Food cooked by this method should be of good quality and very fresh.

Poaching is an excellent way to prepare foods that are to be served cold, as they remain juicy and tender. Foods that are to be served in aspic should be poached; the poaching liquid is reduced and used as a basis for the aspic.

Steaming Fish

All flat fish can be steamed, also many round fish. Very dry-fleshed fish such as sturgeon and swordfish, groupers,

Quarter-cutting Flat Fish

1 To prepare quarter-cut fillets, lay fish, dark skin up, on a board. Cut off head and tail. Trim fins.

2 Place the fish with its tail end facing you. Cut down to the bone along the length of the fish.

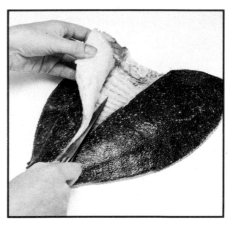

3 To remove the first fillet, work the knife into the cut and gently lift the flesh.

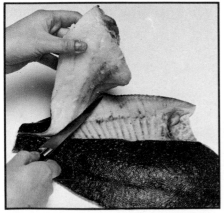

4 With light, stroking movements use the knife to free the fillet from the head end to the tail.

5 To remove the second fillet, turn the fish round and repeat the same action.

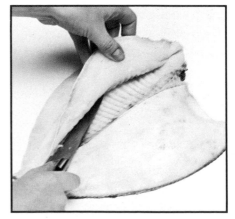

6 Turn the fish over so that the white skin is facing upwards. Remove 2 remaining fillets.

perch, shark and catfish are better cooked by other methods. Cod, haddock, halibut, flounders, shad, sea bass, drums, trout and rockfish are all good possibilities for steaming. These may be filleted or cut into steaks or small pieces. Some fish may be steamed whole; the Chinese have many such preparations, including some for carp, sea bass and snappers. In American markets, flounders, including those called "sole" even if they are not, are sold filleted and completely skinned. If you catch your own, you will need to prepare them—fillet them and skin them. If the fish are sizable, you will need to quartercut them to have smaller fillets. Other fish may be sold already cut into steaks. For some recipes you will need to cut either fillets or steaks into pieces, cutting across the fillets to make strips about 1½ inches wide, or dividing steaks into halves. Even though the Chinese often steam fish with the heads on, for easier serving, remove the heads, skin and bones. Heads and bones can be used for stock.

The liquid used for steaming can be plain water or water flavored with herbs or even court bouillon. Flavored steam will improve the fish. Arrange the steamer pan: a set of Chinese steamer baskets can be set in a wok; a tiny stainless-steel basket steamer can be set in a saucepan; a standard fish poacher with a rack raised up from the bottom; a roasting pan with a cake rack set in the bottom. You can even steam in a colander set in a kettle, or in a clam or vegetable steamer. Pour the liquid into the bottom; use enough liquid so it does not evaporate before steaming is finished, but the liquid must be below the level of the basket.

Prepare the fish. If you are using a Chinese basket steamer or a cake rack, you must set the fish on a plate or double sheet of foil. The plate or foil must be lightly oiled; even the metal steamer basket or the rack of a poacher should be lightly oiled. Metal is a better conductor of heat, but a heavy pottery soup plate or enamelware plate will serve very well. Season the fish on both sides with salt and white pepper

Steaming: Bamboo Basket

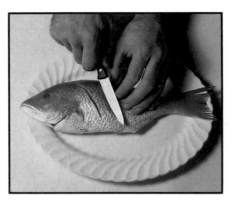

1 *For fish:* Cut 2 diagonal slashes on each side of dressed fish; rub slits with seasoning.

2 Set fish on oiled plate and put plate into basket. Place steamer basket over boiling water in wok. Pour on flavored cooking liquid.

3 Cover basket and steam according to time specified in recipe.

4 Remove basket from wok. Open basket, and tip to lift out plate, being sure to grasp plate with heatproof mitt.

Chopstick Method

1 Fill wok with 2 cups of water. Place 3 chopsticks inside wok, so that they cross to form a center triangle.

2 Place fish on oiled plate, and set plate on top of chopsticks. Cover wok, and steam according to recipe instructions.

Chef's Steamer

1 Pour liquid into bottom of steamer, keeping level below basket. Grease basket; place food on top to cook.

shortly before cooking begins; you may also sprinkle it with minced scallion, fennel leaves, herbs, lemon juice, ginger juice, soy sauce or other flavorings.

Bring the steaming liquid to a boil and set the heat so the liquid steams steadily when the pot is covered; just a little steam should escape from under the cover. If you start the steaming after the fish is in place, the water will froth up and may actually boil the fish. When the steaming is steady, set the rack in place, with the fish on it or on a plate. You must cover the fish if there is no tight cover to the pot. Place another plate upside down on it, or fold the foil over it. In a pot with a snug cover you do not need to do this. The steam will rise to the lid, condense on it, and drop back onto the plate holding the fish. These juices can be used to flavor sauces. In a fish poacher, the juices will drain into the liquid, so the liquid should be saved for sauce making.

If you are using a tiered Chinese basket steamer, other foods can be cooked in the other tiers at the same time, thus saving fuel and time. Or, in a large container such as a colander, fish and other foods can be wrapped loosely in foil and several of these packages can be steamed at the same time.

Small strips of fish, set in a single layer in the steamer, will be fully cooked in 5 minutes. Fillets of thin fish will be perfectly cooked in less than 8 minutes; fatter fillets may take up to 15 minutes, but do not let them cook even 1 minute too long. A fish steak 1 inch thick will be fully cooked in 10 to 12 minutes; if you have cooked it with the bone in, gently test around the bone to be sure it is done; when cooked the bone can be lifted out easily.

Whole small fish such as trout will be cooked in 15 minutes; test near the bone to be sure; these fish may be steamed with their heads still in place. Large whole fish (practical only if you have a large steamer) may be prepared in 2 ways. First, split these fish through the stomach to the backbone to make a single flat piece. This cooks like a fillet, in about 15 minutes. Or, after dressing the fish, cut slashes diagonally on both sides; for a fish of 2 pounds, cut 2 slashes on each side. This allows heat to penetrate to the center more rapidly. Rub some of the seasoning or flavoring in these slashes and on the inside of the fish. Such a fish will be done in 15 to 20 minutes. A large fish such as a 3-pound shad may be steamed for 1½ hours; the long cooking will help soften the bones and make it easier to separate bones from flesh. For such long steaming, be sure to put scallions, slivers of gingerroot or other flavorings into the fish.

If you are steaming fish to serve cold, be sure to remove it from steamer as soon as it is done, and open the foil or remove cover so remaining steam escapes; you do not want the fish to continue to cook. As soon as the fish is cool, cover it to prevent drying.

En Papillote

This is a special kind of steaming, or oven-poaching. The fish is wrapped in a foil or parchment envelope, which is not opened until it reaches the table. The delicious odor of the cooked fish with its accompanying flavors (herbs, sauce, etc.), is part of the delight of this preparation.

The same fish used for steaming can be cooked *en papillote*, except for the large pieces or whole large fish.

The word *papillote* is related to the French word for butterfly, and the opened case looks a little like a butterfly with its wings open. The cases can be cut like a large heart or simply cut into a large rectangle. Foil is an excellent alternative to the original cooking parchment. The foil should be a double thickness twice the size of the fish. Butter or oil the foil; use oil if fish will be served cold.

Place fish on one side of the foil and garnish with a savory butter—anchovy, anise, mustard or orange butter; season with salt and pepper, paprika; flavor with any herbs. Often mushrooms, scallions or minced shallots are arranged on the fish. Lemon juice, wine, vermouth, a few drops of Pernod or Ricard, ginger juice—any of these can be added in small amounts. If you like, the whole meal can be cooked in the packet—the potatoes and other vegetables (but not green vegetables) can be steamed along with the fish. Small fish such as butterfish, porgies or spots can be stuffed and cooked whole in the envelopes.

When the packets are ready, fold the opposite side over and crimp and twist the edges all around to seal them. Place packets on a large baking sheet and slide into a preheated 375°F oven. Bake for 15 to 30 minutes, depending on the thickness of the fish in the parcel.

These dishes are best served hot. If you wish to serve them cold, open them to prevent further cooking. When cool, cover again to prevent drying.

Steaming Poultry

The same principles apply to all steaming, but nothing cooks as quickly as fish, so you must allow more time for all the other foods.

To steam whole chicken or duck, wash the bird well and dry inside and out. Remove any excess fat from the cavity and sprinkle inside well with salt; other seasoning, wine or ginger can be

Steaming: En Papillote

1 To make the case, fold piece of parchment or aluminum foil in half, crosswise. Cut out heart shape, as if for valentine.

2 Butter the center of the case. Make as many cases as needed.

3 Place food on half of buttered parchment or foil near the fold. Arrange mushrooms, herbs or other flavorings on top.

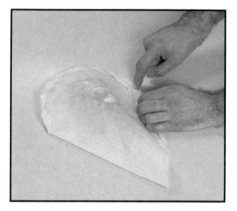

4 When case is filled, carefully crimp edges all around to ensure tight seal.

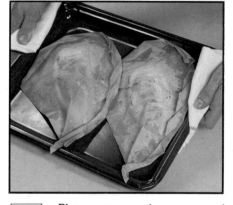

5 Place cases on large, greased baking sheet in preheated oven. Cook according to specific recipe instructions.

6 Transfer cases to heated serving plates. Snip about three quarters of paper on the curved edges. Serve at once.

---

used also. Truss the bird; tie legs together around the tail and fold wings akimbo. Fold skin over the neck opening and fasten with a small skewer. Set bird in the metal steamer basket or on a plate in a bamboo steamer and steam for 45 minutes, or until tender. Duck will require 2 hours; season and flavor a duck at least 1 hour before you start to steam it.

Easier and quicker to steam are pieces of various kinds of poultry. Cut skinned chicken into chunks with a cleaver, including pieces of bone. Duck is better sectioned without bones. Another good choice is to bone chicken breasts completely, cut them into large cubes, and steam with mushrooms and gingerroot. The pieces should be steamed in 30 minutes; test to be sure.

Chicken breasts are tender enough to be cooked *en papillote*. Flavor them with shallots, mushrooms and herbs. They will need more time than fish, but will remain moist and tender even after longer cooking.

Poaching Fish

This is the best general method for all fish and the ideal method for some, such as whole salmon. Poaching does not break up the flesh of the fish, and it does not make the kitchen smell of fish.

As with steaming, use absolutely fresh fish. Choose the liquid: it may be water, water flavored with a generous bunch of herbs or crab boil, available in the spice section of most supermarkets; brine or various kinds of court bouillon (with or without wine, made with vinegar or milk); or fish stock. Prepare the poaching liquid first. Let water or other liquid simmer with the flavoring ingredients for at least 30 minutes. Crab boil or other spices can be tied in

Court Bouillon (Poaching Liquid)

Classic

Makes 1 quart

3 cups water
2 cups dry white wine
2 large onions, chopped
1 carrot, chopped
2 celery ribs, sliced
1 bouquet garni (thyme, parsley, bay leaf)
8 white peppercorns, coarsely crushed
½ teaspoon salt

Combine all ingredients in a large pot; simmer, uncovered, for 1 hour. Cool and strain before using.

White (Milk)

Makes 1 quart

2 cups water
1 cup milk
2 lemon slices
1 teaspoon salt
2 white peppercorns, cracked

Combine all ingredients in a large pot or fish poacher. It is not necessary to simmer this before using it to poach fish.

Vinegar

Makes 1 quart

1 quart water
½ cup red-wine vinegar
1 medium-size onion, chopped
1 carrot, chopped
1 celery rib, chopped
8 white peppercorns, crushed
½ teaspoon salt

Combine all ingredients in a large pot; simmer for 1 hour. Cool and strain before using.

1 A classic court bouillon is made with dry white wine, bouquet garni, carrot, celery, onions and seasonings.

2 A milk court bouillon is suitable for smoked or white-fleshed fish. Cook in a glass or enamel-covered pot.

3 A court bouillon made with red-wine vinegar is best suited to a strong-flavored, oily fish.

a cheesecloth bag, to be lifted out; or the finished court bouillon can be strained. If the flavoring consists of large pieces of vegetables, they can be removed later with a skimmer. Let the finished liquid cool. It is important to start poaching fish in room-temperature liquid; then the entire fish will be heated slowly. If you were to put the fish in hot or boiling liquid, the outer portions would cook almost at once, eventually become overcooked, and the skin would burst.

Rinse the dressed fish, whether a whole fish or large section, fillet or steak. Pat dry and set on a plate. Sprinkle with a little lemon juice, ginger juice or herbs. Do not salt fish that is to be poached, as the salt will dissolve in the liquid. Instead, add salt to the poaching liquid to season the fish as it cooks. Use ½ to 1 teaspoon for each quart of water. Let fish absorb the flavors for up to 30 minutes.

If you are working with a large fish, place it on an oiled poaching rack. Lacking a fish poacher, arrange fish on an oiled sheet of foil on an improvised rack (a cake rack) in a large roasting pan, placing a long fish from corner to corner if it is too long to fit any other way. Work out some method to lift the improvised rack from the pan. If you have a fish with soft texture such as bluefish, or any fish that seems fragile, wrap it from end to end in cheesecloth and tie the ends. This makes it possible to lift it out without breaking it. If you are serving the fish cold, you will find it less fragile after cooling.

Lower the rack into the pan or poacher and pour in room-temperature liquid just to cover the fish. Cover the pan. If you have no cover, improvise with foil. Over low heat bring the liquid to a simmer and cook for the time required. The time depends on the thickness of the fish. Allow 10 minutes per inch, measured at the thickest part. If you are serving the fish cold, let it cool in the poaching liquid.

If you are working with steaks or fillets, you will not need a large fish poacher. Steaks or fillets can be cooked in a large skillet or any flat pan large enough to hold them in a single

Poaching Fish: 2 Methods

layer. Butter the skillet and sprinkle it with chopped onion or shallot, some roughly chopped parsley and a tiny piece of bay leaf. If you have boned pieces, add bones to the pan for greater flavor and for the gelatin they will release. Set prepared steaks or thick fillets on this bed. They may be flavored and seasoned; use salt lightly. Gently pour in room-temperature liquid, which for this may be as simple as half wine and half water; fish stock, lemon juice, tomato juice, celery or mushroom broth can be used in place of wine. The choice depends on the kind of sauce you plan to make, as this poaching liquid will be part of the sauce. The liquid should barely reach the top of the fish pieces. Butter a piece of foil or kitchen parchment, make a hole in the center for steam to escape, and press it, buttered side down, on the fish. Bring liquid to a boil, cover the pan, and poach (simmer, not boil) for the needed time. Small whole fish such as trout that weigh 8 to 10 ounces should be done in about 15 minutes. Steaks and thick fillets will need about 12 minutes.

When fish is done, lift it out with a flat skimmer to a thick plate and keep it warm. Reduce the poaching liquid to three quarters or half, strain it, and whisk in some butter; or thicken with a liaison of egg yolk and cream. Or make a butter-flour roux and pour in the liquid to make a sauce.

Following this basic method and varying the garnish of vegetables, fruits and herbs, you can make dozens of different dishes with fish steaks and fillets.

Poaching Salmon, Trout and Smoked Fish

Salmon is the perfect fish for poaching; this may be the best way to prepare it. Large trout are also good this way. Have the fish whole-dressed (head, tail and fins remain in place). It should be absolutely fresh. Buy 8 to 10 ounces of whole fish per serving to allow for loss in bones and head. Plan to poach the fish the day you buy it.

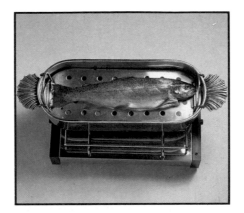

1 When using a poacher, place whole-dressed fish on a greased rack.

2 Lower rack into room-temperature court bouillon. Cover; bring to a simmer and cook for time required; do not overcook.

3 Lift rack with cooked fish from liquid. Transfer to warmed serving platter. Or, if serving cold, let fish cool in liquid.

OR Wrap fish in double thickness of cheesecloth; tie ends securely. Lower into court bouillon. Cover; bring to a simmer.

When fish is tender and the liquid has cooled to warm, lift out the still-warm fish to a thick layer of folded cloth towel. Make a cut just above the tail and another around the head and top end of the fish. Starting at the tail, gently pull off the skin. If the fish is still warm, it will be easy to do. Scrape off the upper layer of darker meat on the salmon, especially the line along the spine. This is edible but spoils the appearance. Remove the eye. Turn fish over, using the cloth to help, and repeat the process on the other side. Gently separate the halves and remove the backbone. Reassemble the fish and

transfer to a serving platter. It is now ready to be cooled completely, coated with aspic, and garnished; or it can be served warm with a hot sauce.

Blue trout (truite au bleu) are whole small trout dropped into boiling court bouillon. From that point on the liquid never boils; when it reaches the boiling point after trout are added, the kettle is removed from heat, covered, and left to stand for about 20 minutes. Blue trout are served curled; dropping them into boiling liquid causes the backbone and skin to shrink, so the whole little fish is bent around. This works only with freshly caught trout

38

Skinning and Boning Poached Whole Salmon

1 Lay salmon on a folded cloth towel (first choice) or on a large sheet of greaseproof paper.

2 With a sharp knife cut the skin across the tail, around the head, and along the top of the fish.

3 Peel the skin away, using the knife to help. If the fish is still warm, it will be easy to do this.

4 Scrape off the dark flesh and the brown strip along the backbone. These spoil the appearance.

5 Use cloth or paper to help turn the fish over. Repeat skinning and scraping on the underside.

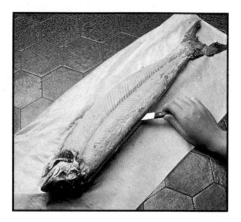

6 Slide the knife under the upper fillet, flat against the bone, to separate bone and flesh.

7 Using 2 flat turners, lift off the upper fillet and lay it on the cloth or paper.

8 Snip through the backbone at both head and tail ends and peel it away from the fish. Remove any loose bones as well.

9 Carefully lift the upper fillet, or 2 half fillets, back into place to reassemble the fish. Transfer to a platter and garnish.

which have not been washed or scaled. Gut fish quickly, then dip them into a hot bath of one third vinegar and two thirds water, which preserves the color of the skin. Then drop into the boiling court bouillon.

Poaching Poultry

Some of the most delicious chicken dishes start out with a large roaster or fowl poached in flavored water. Small birds may also be cooked this way. Capon, duck and goose are excellent poached; in fact for the fattier birds it may be the best cooking method since the fat is extracted and the meat remains tender.

Truss the dressed bird. Chickens and small poultry may be stuffed if you like. If it is a large older bird, blanch it, starting in cold water, for 5 minutes first. Drain the bird, wash the kettle, and start again in water, or water and stock mixed. Add flavoring vegetables (carrot, onion, celery, leek) and herbs if you like. Bring to a boil and skim as needed. Reduce to a bare simmer, cov-

er, and poach for about 2 hours for a bird of 5 pounds or more. If you have used stock for cooking, you will have a flavorful soup; or some of the cooking liquid can be used to make a velouté sauce.

If you plan to make a cold chicken dish, let the bird cool in the cooking liquid; it will be more juicy and flavorful.

Small chickens can be poached the same way, but they need only 45 minutes or less to be tender, and they need no blanching. Be sure to truss them before cooking.

Poaching Chicken

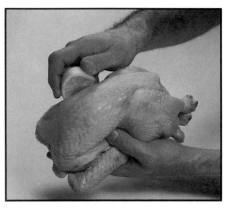 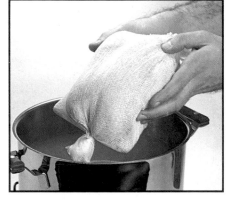 

1 Rub unstuffed, whole chicken with lemon. Wrap and tie chicken in double thickness of cheesecloth.

2 Immerse bird in cold water; bring to simmer, uncovered, skimming when necessary.

3 When cooked in accordance with recipe instructions, remove cooked chicken from poaching liquid, using 2 slotted spoons.

Poaching Chicken in Vegetable Broth

 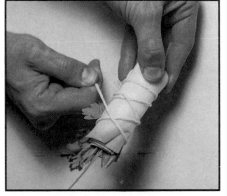 

1 Assemble a bouquet garni by using a cleaned leek as a container to hold fresh and dried herbs.

2 Secure the bouquet garni by criss-crossing white string around leek several times.

3 Proceed to poach chicken, following specific recipe for cooking time. Degrease vegetable broth at end of cooking time.

Tilefish Poached in Cider

4 portions

1 medium-size onion
1 large carrot
2 tablespoons unsalted
  butter
1¼ cups tart cider

4 tilefish fillets, about 6
  ounces each
1 cup Beurre Blanc (see
  Index)

Peel onion and cut into thin slices. Scrape and slice the carrot. Melt the butter in a large skillet over low heat. When foam subsides, add onion and carrot. Sauté, stirring occasionally, until onion is translucent. Pour in the cider and bring to a boil. Lay tilefish fillets in the pan and poach for 8 to 10 minutes, until fish flakes easily. Lift the fillets to a warmed serving dish. With a skimmer lift the slices of onion and carrot and arrange around the fish. Sprinkle a little of the cider over each fillet. Serve the *beurre blanc* separately in a warmed sauceboat.

Dilled Salmon en Papillote

4 portions

4 tablespoons unsalted
  butter
4 salmon steaks, Atlantic or
  Chinook, about 5
  ounces each

  salt and white pepper
2 hard-cooked eggs
1 bunch of fresh dill
  fresh lemon juice

Preheat oven to 450°F. Cut 4 pieces of aluminum foil or parchment paper into 14-inch squares. Coat the center of each square with 1 tablespoon of the butter. Place 1 salmon steak on each square. Sprinkle with salt and white pepper. Shell and chop the eggs and divide them among the steaks. Top each one with 2 or 3 sprigs of dill. Sprinkle with a little lemon juice.

Fold the foil or parchment over the salmon and crimp the edges to seal. Place the packages on baking sheets. Bake them in the preheated oven for 13 to 15 minutes. Serve the salmon in the packets. Each person opens his packet or *papillote* at the table, just before eating.

Circassian Chicken

6 portions

1 roasting chicken, 5 pounds
1 onion
1 carrot
1 celery rib
3 parsley sprigs
1 bay leaf

  salt
10 peppercorns
2 quarts water
10 ounces shelled walnuts
2½ cups fresh white bread crumbs
¾ cup light cream

Remove giblets from the chicken and set aside for another use. Rinse chicken and put it in a large kettle. Add the onion, carrot, celery, parsley sprigs, bay leaf, ½ teaspoon salt, the peppercorns and the 2 quarts water. Bring the water to a boil over high heat, then reduce heat, cover the chicken, and simmer gently for 1 to 1½ hours, until chicken tests tender when pierced with a knife.

While the chicken is being poached, prepare the sauce. Grind walnuts in a blender or crush them in a food mill. Put walnuts in a large mixing bowl with the bread crumbs. When the chicken is cooked, remove ¾ cup of the cooking liquid and pour it through a strainer into the bowl of walnuts and crumbs. Stir in the cream and add ½ teaspoon salt. If the sauce is too thick, add a little more of the strained cooking liquid. Taste, and season more if necessary.

Remove chicken from the kettle. With a sharp knife cut chicken into portions or slices. Place on a warmed serving dish and pour a little of the sauce over. Serve remaining sauce in a warmed bowl. Serve at once.

Blue Trout

4 portions

4	live trout, each 8 to 10 ounces	2	quarts Classic Court Bouillon (see Index)
1½	cups white-wine vinegar	2	lemons
2½	cups water	6	parsley sprigs
		¾	cup clarified butter

Handling the trout with wet hands, and touching them as little as possible, kill the trout with a sharp blow at the back of the head. Gut the fish, but do not remove fins, heads or scales. Combine the white-wine vinegar and water and bring to a boil. Pick up each trout with tongs, holding it by the head, and lower it into the vinegar. It will turn blue from the reaction of vinegar on the natural coating of the skin. Bring the court bouillon to a boil and lower the trout into it. When the bouillon comes again to a boil, remove the kettle from heat and let it stand for 15 to 20 minutes, the longer time for larger fish.

Quarter the lemons and mince the parsley. Heat the clarified butter over low heat. When the trout are ready, lift them from the kettle to a serving platter. Tilt the platter to drain off any remaining court bouillon and mop up around the fish with absorbent paper. Sprinkle parsley over the fish and garnish with lemon wedges. Serve the melted butter in a sauceboat. Serve trout and butter immediately.

Sole Véronique

4 portions

8 fillets of sole, 4 ounces each	½ cup Béchamel Sauce (see Index), hot
salt and white pepper	2 large egg yolks
2 cups strong fish stock (fumet)	¼ cup heavy cream
4 ounces seedless white grapes	2 tablespoons butter, softened

Season the fillets with salt and white pepper and lay them flat in a shallow flameproof dish. Pour in enough of the *fumet* to cover the fish. Bring the liquid to a simmer and adjust heat to maintain a bare simmer. Poach the fillets for 6 to 8 minutes.

Pick grapes from their stems and drop them into a bowl of near-boiling water to heat through. After a few minutes, lift grapes out of the water with a perforated spoon. Lift fillets out of the *fumet* with a perforated spatula; let them drain well over the dish, then transfer them to a serving platter; keep fish warm. Drain grapes well and arrange around the fish.

Taste the *fumet* in the cooking vessel; if it is not strong-tasting, reduce it to concentrate the flavor. Measure 1 cup of the *fumet* and strain it into the hot béchamel sauce. In a small bowl beat the egg yolks and 2 tablespoons of the cream together to make a liaison. Add 4 tablespoons of the hot sauce to the liaison, stirring all the while. Stir into the rest of the sauce. Heat the sauce over low heat, stirring, until it thickens. Set the pan over hot water to keep warm. Preheat the broiler.

Whip remaining cream until thick but not stiff. Stir the softened butter into the hot sauce, then fold in the whipped cream. Pour the sauce over the fish and grapes. Place under the broiler for 1 minute to brown the top, and serve immediately.

Poached Chicken with Broccoli

4 portions

1 roasting chicken, 4 pounds	½ teaspoon grated nutmeg
6 cups water	½ cup heavy cream
salt	¾ cup Hollandaise Sauce (see Index)
1½ pounds broccoli	
4 tablespoons butter	3 tablespoons sherry
3 tablespoons flour	3 ounces Parmesan cheese, grated (about ½ cup)
2 cups milk	

Remove the package of giblets from the chicken and set aside for another use. Fold the wings under the backbone and tie the legs together. Put chicken in a large kettle with 6 cups water and 2 teaspoons salt. Bring the water to a boil over high heat, then reduce heat and poach the chicken for 1 hour, or until it is tender. Remove pan from heat and let the chicken cool in the cooking liquid.

Wash and trim the broccoli; separate into florets and peel the stems. Put broccoli in a large saucepan, sprinkle with 1 teaspoon salt, and cover with cold water. Bring to a boil, then simmer for about 8 minutes, until broccoli is crisp-tender. Drain, rinse with ice water to set the color, and drain again.

Make white sauce: Melt the butter in a medium-size saucepan over moderate heat. Remove pan from heat and with a wooden spoon stir in the flour to make a smooth paste. Gradually add the milk, stirring constantly. Return pan to heat and cook, stirring, for 2 to 3 minutes, until sauce is thick and smooth. Remove pan from heat and stir in the nutmeg; set aside. Beat the heavy cream to the mousse stage, thick but not stiff. Stir the hollandaise sauce into the white sauce. Using a metal spatula, fold the cream and the sherry into the sauce; set aside.

Preheat oven to 375°F. When the chicken is cool enough to handle, transfer it to a chopping board. (The cooking liquid may be refrigerated to use for soups and other dishes.) Discard skin and cut chicken into serving pieces or slices.

Arrange the broccoli in a large ovenproof serving dish. Sprinkle half of the grated cheese over broccoli. Arrange chicken pieces on top of the cheese. Pour the sauce over the chicken and sprinkle with remaining cheese. Bake chicken and broccoli in the preheated oven for 30 minutes, until the top is golden brown. Remove dish from the oven and serve.

Pai Chiu Tung Li Yu

(Carp Steamed in White Wine)

4 to 6 portions

1 carp, 3 pounds	3 tablespoons soy sauce
1 cup water	1½ tablespoons sesame seed oil
1 cup fish stock	1 bunch of watercress (optional)
1½ cups dry white wine	

Stuffing

¼ cup uncooked long-grain rice	3— inch piece of fresh gingerroot
4 slices of lean bacon	1 chicken bouillon cube
4 green onions (scallions)	¼ teaspoon salt
	¼ teaspoon white pepper

Have the carp scaled and skinned, gutted and fins removed; leave head and tail in place. Make the stuffing for the carp: Wash the rice, soak in cold water for 30 minutes, then drain. Chop the bacon. Trim and chop green onions, both white and green parts. Peel and mince the gingerroot. In a medium-size bowl combine rice, bacon, green onions, gingerroot, the bouillon cube, crushed, and salt and pepper. Stuff the mixture into the carp and close the opening with skewers or sew with a trussing needle and thread. Place carp in a shallow oval flameproof casserole large enough to hold it and pour in 1 cup water. Pour enough water into the bottom of a large steamer to reach a depth of 2 inches. Place the casserole over the steamer and cover it. Set the steamer over moderate heat and steam for 45 minutes. Pour the stock and wine into the casserole and continue to steam for another 45 minutes, until fish flakes when tested with a fork.

Remove steamer from the heat and the casserole from the steamer. Using slotted spoons, lift the carp to a warmed oval serving platter. Keep the carp warm. Remove skewers or trussing strings. Combine soy sauce and sesame seed oil and blend with a fork. Pour the mixture over the fish. Garnish the platter with watercress and serve at once.

If you like, the cooking liquid from the casserole can be used for soup. Chop a bunch of watercress and cook it in the boiling liquid for 2 minutes. Serve in bowls as a first course.

Chinese Steamed Rockfish

*The method used is the same as that for steaming whole
carp, but here only fillets are steamed.*

2 portions

2 fillets of rockfish or red
    snapper, 6 to 8 ounces
    each
    salt and pepper
4 ounces mushrooms
2 green onions (scallions)

1 garlic clove
1 teaspoon cornstarch
2 tablespoons soy sauce
4 tablespoons sesame oil
1 tablespoon wine vinegar
¼ teaspoon sugar

Select a plate that is large enough to hold the fillets in a single layer and that will fit in a steamer. Place fillets on the plate and sprinkle with salt and pepper. Wipe the mushrooms with a damp cloth and trim the base of the stems. Cut mushrooms into thick slices and add to the fish. Trim green onions and chop both white and green parts; put in a bowl. Peel garlic and put through a press into the onions. Blend cornstarch with soy sauce and add to onions. Stir in sesame oil, vinegar, sugar and some pepper. Mix well and pour the mixture over the fish. Cover the plate with another lightly oiled plate or a sheet of oiled foil. Set over the steamer and steam for 10 to 15 minutes. Serve at once, with steamed rice and green beans cooked with gingerroot.

Poached Haddock, Hot and Cold

Poached Haddock, Hot

4 portions

1 whole haddock, 4 to 5
    pounds
2 quarts Classic Court
    Bouillon (see Index)

1 large egg
4 parsley sprigs
2 tablespoons butter
1 lemon

Have the fish whole-dressed at the market. Measure the fish at the thickest part. Allow 10 minutes per inch for the poaching time. Wipe fish inside and out with damp paper towels, then place on a thick layer of cheesecloth longer at both ends than the fish; the extra length will serve as handles when lifting out the fish. Lift the fish into a fish poacher, or use a roasting pan with the fish arranged from corner to corner. Pour in enough of the cool court bouillon to cover the fish; if 2 quarts is not enough (due to the size and shape of the pan), add enough cool water to cover fish. Bring the liquid to a simmer and adjust to remain at a bare simmer. Poach for 10 minutes per inch, or until almost tender. The haddock will remain in the court bouillon and finish cooking in the retained heat of the liquid; at the same time it will become more flavorful and juicy.

Hard-cook the egg, plunge into cold water; and shell it. Chop egg and parsley, then chop them together to mix well.

Lift the fish to a board and pat dry. Skin the upper surface and trim the fins on both sides. Cut down along the backbone and carefully lift off the 2 upper fillets. Place them close together on a serving platter to approximate the original shape of the fish. Melt the butter over low heat and brush it over the haddock. Cut the lemon into very thin slices and arrange the slices down the center to cover the joining of the 2 fillets. Scatter the chopped egg and parsley over and serve immediately.

Poached Haddock, Cold

4 portions

1 large egg
2 parsley sprigs
6 tarragon leaves
12 chive leaves
5 shelled walnuts

6 capers
¾ cup vinaigrette dressing
    lemon slices
    watercress sprigs

Carefully remove fins, bone, head and tail from the rest of the haddock. Let the fillets cool, then cover with foil and refrigerate.

When ready to serve the cold haddock, arrange the fillets on a shallow serving platter to approximate the shape of the fish. Hard-cook the egg, plunge into cold water, and shell. Chop the egg. Wash and dry the herbs and snip with scissors into very small bits. Chop the walnuts. Mix egg, herbs, capers and walnuts into the vinaigrette dressing. Check the seasoning, then pour vinaigrette over the fish. Serve at once, or cover lightly and chill. Although the haddock can be served ice cold, it is more flavorful when only cool. For a final garnish use paper-thin slices of lemon and watercress sprigs.

Skate with Black Butter

4 portions

2½ pounds skate
1 quart Vinegar Court Bouillon (see Index)
2 tablespoons chopped fresh parsley

6 tablespoons unsalted butter
2 tablespoons white-wine vinegar

Cut skate into portions to fit into a large shallow pan. Pour in enough of the court bouillon to cover the fish; if more liquid is needed, add water. Slowly bring the liquid to a simmer and adjust to maintain a bare simmer. Cover the pan and poach the skate for 8 to 15 minutes, depending on thickness; it should be tender.

Transfer skate to a board and remove any skin and the bone. Cut into serving portions. Place the fish on a warmed serving platter and keep it warm. Sprinkle parsley over the skate.

Melt the butter in a heavy skillet over low heat. Heat it until it foams and begins to turn a deep golden brown. At once pour it over the skate. Pour vinegar into the skillet, heat for 1 minute, and pour that also over the skate. Serve immediately.

Cod Fillets with Caper Cream Sauce

4 portions

8 small cod fillets, skinned	1 teaspoon cornstarch
3 cups Classic Court	dissolved in 1
Bouillon (see Index)	tablespoon water
8 large shrimps in shells,	pinch of cayenne pepper
about 8 ounces	¾ cup heavy cream
1 teaspoon crab boil or	2 tablespoons capers
pickling spices	

Roll up the cod fillets and fasten the rolls with thick thread. Lay the rolls in the bottom of a heavy saucepan. Pour in the court bouillon. Set the pan over moderate heat and bring the liquid to a boil. Reduce heat, cover the pan, and simmer for 20 minutes. Remove pan from heat.

While the fish is being poached, wash shrimps and cover with water in a saucepan. Add crab boil or pickling spices. Bring to a boil and cook for about 6 minutes, until shrimps are pink. Drain and rinse to remove any bits of spice.

Lift fish rolls from the pan to a heated serving dish.

Remove the threads from the rolls. Keep fish hot. Return the saucepan to high heat and boil the cooking juices until they are reduced to half the original volume. Stir in dissolved cornstarch and cayenne. Cook sauce for about 3 minutes, until thickened. Stir in the cream and capers and continue to cook, stirring constantly, for 3 minutes longer, until the sauce almost comes to a boil. Remove from heat at once and pour over the fish. Garnish with the shrimps, still in their shells, and serve at once.

Poule-au-Pot

(Chicken-in-the-Pot)

4 portions

1 roasting chicken, 3 pounds	1 tablespoon olive oil
2 tablespoons chopped fresh	1 tablespoon butter
tarragon	1 bouquet garni
1 small strip of lemon rind	10 ounces new potatoes
salt and pepper	1 pound young leeks
1 large carrot	8 ounces green snap beans
2 or 3 celery ribs	1 cup vinaigrette dressing
1 large onion	

Remove the giblets from the chicken cavity, rinse it well, and pat dry. Place the chopped tarragon and lemon rind in the cavity of the chicken together with a good amount of salt and pepper. Scrub the carrot, wash and chop the celery, and peel the onion and cut into quarters. Use a heavy pot that will hold the chicken snugly. Heat the oil and butter in the pot. Fold the chicken wings under the back and tie the legs together. Put the bird in the heated pot and sauté it on all sides until the skin is pale gold. Lift the chicken out of the pot. Put into the pot the carrot, celery and onion. Return the chicken, placing it on top of the vegetables. Add the *bouquet garni* and pour in enough hot water to cover the chicken thighs. Bring the water quickly to a boil, then reduce heat, cover the pot, and simmer gently for 1 hour.

Meanwhile prepare the other vegetables and make the vinaigrette. About 30 minutes before the chicken is ready, start steaming the new potatoes. Add the whole leeks about 10 minutes later, the beans after a further 8 minutes. All the vegetables can be cooked in the same steamer basket. When the chicken is ready, turn off the heat but leave chicken in the pot.

Arrange the steamed vegetables around the edge of a large warmed serving dish and moisten them with a few tablespoons of the broth from the pot. Drain the chicken, cut into 4 portions, and place the portions in the center of the serving dish. Serve the vinaigrette in a sauceboat.

Steamed Sole with Chive and Cucumber Sauce

4 portions

4 sole fillets, 5 or 6 ounces
   each, skinned
   vegetable oil
   salt and white pepper
   juice of ½ lemon
½ small cucumber

4 tablespoons unsalted
   butter
2 tablespoons flour
1 cup milk
2 tablespoons snipped fresh
   chives

Select a heatproof plate large enough to hold the fillets in a single layer; the plate must be slightly larger than the saucepan or skillet used for steaming. Lightly oil the plate and a large piece of foil. Arrange the fillets on the plate; sprinkle with salt, pepper and lemon juice. Fold in both ends of each fillet to make a threefold packet. Cover the plate tightly with foil. (At this point, the fish may be refrigerated until ready to cook.)

Fill the chosen saucepan or skillet half full with water. Bring water to a boil and place the plate of fish over the pan. Cover the plate and steam the fish for 10 to 15 minutes, or until the thickest part of the fillet is opaque.

Meanwhile make the sauce: Peel and dice the cucumber. Cook in 2 tablespoons of the butter for 5 minutes. Melt remaining butter in a separate saucepan. Reduce heat to low and stir in the flour; stir for 1 minute. Remove pan from heat and gradually stir in the milk. Return saucepan to heat and stir until the sauce is boiling. Keep covered over low heat.

Transfer the cooked fillets to a warmed serving platter. Pour the fish juices from the plate into the sauce. Add sautéed cucumber, the chives, and seasoning to taste. Pour sauce over fish and serve at once.

Chicken Salad with Walnuts, Grapes and Tarragon

4 to 6 portions

1 roasting chicken, 4 pounds
1 teaspoon salt
3 tarragon sprigs
2 tablespoons unsalted
   butter
½ cup dry white wine
½ cup water
1 teaspoon dry mustard
½ teaspoon sugar

½ teaspoon freshly ground
   black pepper
6 tablespoons olive oil
2 tablespoons vinegar
¼ cup light cream
1 pound green grapes
1 teaspoon dried tarragon
1 head of romaine
¾ cup chopped walnuts

Preheat oven to 350°F. Rub inside of chicken with ½ teaspoon of the salt. Put tarragon sprigs and 1 tablespoon of the butter in the cavity of the chicken. Rub remaining butter over the skin of the chicken. Place chicken, wine and water in a Dutch oven; cover tightly. Oven-poach the chicken for 1½ to 2 hours, until chicken is tender. Test by piercing a thigh with a skewer; the juices should be clear. Skim fat from the surface of the cooking liquid. Strain liquid into a measuring cup and reserve 5 ounces of it.

Let the chicken cool, then cut it into 8 portions; remove as much bone as practical, and if the portions seem large, divide them into halves. Chill chicken pieces.

Make the sauce: Combine mustard, sugar, remaining ½ teaspoon salt and the pepper in a bowl. Beat in oil, vinegar, cream, and reserved strained cooking juices. Add grapes and tarragon. Wash and trim romaine and separate into leaves. Dry the leaves.

At serving time arrange romaine leaves on a serving dish; top with chicken pieces. Spoon sauce over the chicken and garnish the salad with walnuts.

Mackerel Fillets with Mustard Hollandaise

4 portions

2 mackerels, 1 pound each
  salt and pepper
	1 tablespoon prepared
	  Dijon-style mustard

1 tablespoon lemon juice	2 teaspoons capers

1 cup Hollandaise Sauce
  (see Index)
	2 teaspoons chopped fresh
	  parsley
	  tomato wedges
	  watercress sprigs

Dress and fillet the mackerels, or have the fish market do it. Lay fillets on a piece of oiled aluminum foil. Sprinkle with salt, a little pepper and the lemon juice. Fold over both ends of each fillet to make a packet and wrap each one into a secure parcel. Prepare a steamer and place the parcels in the steamer basket over boiling water. Steam for 20 to 25 minutes, until the fish tests done.

Meanwhile prepare the hollandaise and flavor it with the mustard. Transfer fish to a serving dish and pour the juices into the sauce. Crush the capers and add to the sauce along with the parsley. Gently mix it all together and spoon the sauce over the fish. Garnish with tomato wedges and watercress sprigs. Serve at once.

Pai Chiu Tung Chi

(Chicken Simmered in White Wine)

4 portions

½	cup uncooked long-grain rice	1	roasting chicken, 3½ pounds
4	green onions (scallions)	2½	cups water
4	slices of lean bacon	1¼	cups dry white wine
1	2-inch piece of fresh gingerroot	1	pound Chinese cabbage
1	chicken bouillon cube	3	tablespoons soy sauce
¼	teaspoon salt	1½	tablespoons sesame seed oil
¼	teaspoon freshly ground white pepper		

Soak the rice in cold water for 30 minutes; drain. Trim and chop green onions. Chop bacon. Peel and mince gingerroot. Prepare stuffing: Combine rice, green onions, bacon, gingerroot, bouillon cube, crushed, salt and pepper in a bowl and mix. Stuff cavity of chicken with the mixture and secure the opening with small skewers or sew with thread.

Preheat oven to 350°F. Place chicken and 2½ cups water in a deep flameproof casserole dish. Bring to a boil over medium-high heat on top of the stove. Remove from stove top, cover, and place in the oven. Poach chicken in the oven for 1 hour. Add the wine and poach for 45 minutes more, until chicken is tender.

Transfer chicken to a warmed serving platter. Keep it warm. Remove skewers or trussing strings from chicken. Combine soy sauce and sesame seed oil and pour the mixture over the chicken. Serve at once.

If you like, the cooking liquid can be used for soup. Trim, rinse, and shred Chinese cabbage. Cook cabbage in the poaching liquid over medium heat for 5 minutes. Serve cabbage and broth in bowls as a first course.

Part Three
STUFFED VEGETABLES

There is something about stuffed vegetables that has almost universal appeal. The elemental basic shapes, the blend of textures, colors and tastes speak the providence of nature and the pleasures of a simpler life. Why not replace the china with pretty vine leaves of the grape, or lettuces or green opalescent leaves of cabbages; turn eggplants into shiny purple bowls; stout, sturdy peppers into hollow cups; make pretty ramekins from ruby red tomatoes; transform a golden pumpkin into a soup tureen.

"A garden is a lovesome thing, God wot!" said Edward Thomas Brown sometime between the years of 1830 and 1897. And so it is when it produces a cornucopia of vegetables, bursting with fresh good taste, gleaming with healthful vivid colors and in such copious abundance that even clever and resourceful cooks are challenged to put them all to proper use. In summertime, when vegetables abound, we eat less meat, cut down on fats, and highlight vegetables as they come into season. Among the many ways that vegetables are cooked and eaten, stuffed vegetables have great versatility and much appeal. There is an almost irresistible charm in food that's served in edible containers or wrapped in bundles you can eat.

Stuffed vegetables, like breads or stews or other basic dishes, appear in one form or another all over the world; they are used in vastly diverse cuisines. They were known in the early centuries of the Byzantine Empire, before 1300, and probably date back to the ancient Greeks. Some of the preparations may first appear to be a bit elaborate and some of the fillings call for lavish ingredients, but on the whole, stuffed vegetables are not classified as *haute cuisine*. Most recipes are products of a folk imagination; they represent a practical solution to making the best use of what there is at hand. Like handmade quilts, a recipe combines the virtues of economy, resourceful ingenuity and craft. The recipes of folk cuisine are more than formulaic guides. Like any other good idea, they also serve as inspiration. Do it the way it always has been done, then try some variations of your own.

Claudia Roden describes a way to eat tabbouleh (a splendid summer salad of bulgur, scallions, mint and parsley dressed with fresh lemon juice and olive oil): "(It) is traditionally served in individual plates lined with boiled vine leaves, or raw lettuce or cabbage leaves. People scoop the salad up with more leaves, served in a separate bowl..." *(A Book of Middle Eastern Food)*. This is a practical and delicious idea; the lettuce leaves make natural scoops, and add an element of play along with their cool, crisp texture and pleasing taste. Many variations on this theme are possible: the pale elegant leaves of the aristocratic endive are admirable alternatives to bread or crackers with a dip; crisp, salty celery ribs come ready made to fill with softened cheese or any other savory spread; surround a bowl of homemade mayonnaise with tender leaves of artichokes.

More commonly, the leafy greens of vegetables are used as tasty wrappers to hold an enormous variety of fillings. A glance at the cuisine of other lands shows the astonishing scope and range of vegetable cookery. Take for example the lowly cabbage—a vegetable we have maligned, abused and misunderstood. Not so in France, Austria, Germany, Czechoslovakia, Hungary, Poland or Russia, where cabbage, and particularly the many glorious varieties of stuffed cabbage, rank high among the best of country food. George Lang, in *The Cuisine of Hungary,* devotes an entire chapter to ways of cooking cabbage and claims he has sorted through more than 800 recipes that feature this hardy, toothsome, healthful head of greens.

Indeed, stuffed cabbage leaves are among the most attractive and flavorful of dishes. Each leaf becomes an envelope to hold a savory mixture of grains, forcemeat, mushrooms, herbs...the possibilities for fillings are endless and include not only other vegetables and every sort of grain, but economical, delicious ways to use up the leftover bits of roasts or stews. The cabbage rolls are braised in stock, or in a sauce (hearty tomato; spicy sweet-sour sauce; a béchamel or velouté—these are just a few of the available options). These hearty dishes are comforting to eat and satisfy both dinner guest and cook. They provide the kinds of meals that never overtax your budget or your busy schedule—they are economical to make and always taste better when they have been made a day ahead.

One of the glories of cabbage cookery is the spectacular, dramatic presentation of a whole cabbage head, layered with stuffing between the leaves. This takes a bit more time to do but is not difficult; the results are most impressive.

In warmer climates, the cabbage does not thrive. John Gerard said in his *Herball* back in 1636 "...that there is a naturallenmitie betweene it (cabbage) and the vine...if it grow neere unto it, forthwith the vine perisheth..." But the grape vine itself generously provides in great abundance elegant leaves with a fragrant, pungent flavor. *Dolmades, dolmas, dolmadakia*—all are plump, savory parcels wrapped in the deep green leaves of the beloved grape vine (even though the same names may be used for other stuffed vegetables). In Greece, in Turkey, in all the sunny Mediterranean lands and all across the Middle East, vine leaves are stuffed with rice seasoned with fragrant herbs and dried currants; with spicy lamb and aromatic pine nuts. They can be eaten hot or cold; they make an appetizer or a meal; they please the eye, seduce the palate; and they are irresistibly delicious.

Consider other leafy greens—Swiss chard, lettuces, young tender spinach, peppery nasturtium leaves—as long as they are edible, there is a way to wrap each leaf around a tasty morsel. This kind of culinary play shows off a cook's imagination, creativity and craft.

There are many other vegetables that are excellent for stuffing. Peppers are justly popular; their neat and hollow shape provides a succulent and sturdy cup to fill with a stuffing of your choice. Peppers are most adaptable and can be stuffed when they are raw, or when first blanched, or grilled and skinned. Stuffed peppers take about the same amount of preparation time as it would take to make a meat loaf, but there are days when we would like our food to have a bit more individuality and charm.

The green bell peppers are available year round, but there are seasons when you may also come across peppers that are fire-engine red and others that are a brilliant golden yellow. Then you can be an artist in the kitchen, mixing them in wonderful combinations. Delight your family and friends with colorful mosaics and a variety of tastes.

Certain occasions call for a meal that brings a sense of luxury, an elegance of taste and mood. A lush, ripe avocado or a full, plump artichoke are nature's perfect answers to this need.

The small dark avocados grown in the western states are more intensely flavorful than the larger ones that come from Florida. Whichever variety you choose, allow it to become fully ripe before you serve it. The avocado's delicate taste and velvety texture marries extremely well with crab meat, shrimp, lobster or other kinds of seafood. As in many other luxury dishes, the preparation is simplicity itself. Slice through the avocado, around the pit, and split the fruit. Remove the pit, sprinkle the pale green flesh with lemon or lime juice and fill it up with seafood. Simply divine and divinely simple to prepare.

It's hard to think of a more intriguing vegetable than that described by D. H. Lawrence, "(the) young, purplish, seadust-colored artichoke." Artichokes are particularly elegant containers. The whole of it can be stuffed, in the center and between the rows of leaves, with savory forcemeat, seasoned bread crumbs, or vegetable purées of every sort. Or serve the tender, meaty bottoms filled with tasty mixtures, smooth purées, or even a soufflé.

Tomatoes can be stuffed in many of the same ways as peppers. Some cooks bake an assortment of stuffed peppers and tomatoes in the same dish.

A delicious Italian version stuffs a creamy cheese risotto into the tomato shells; Indians stuff hollowed-out tomatoes with pungent, spiced potatoes.

Mushrooms, their stems removed, make small neat saucers to fill with various ingredients. Small mushroom caps make an excellent hors d'oeuvre when filled with softened cheese and served uncooked, just as they are. The larger mushroom caps (including the delicious wild varieties when you can get them) are stuffed and baked or broiled.

The royal purple eggplant is also stuffed in many ways and found in the cuisines of countries round the world. The taste of eggplants combines with an astonishing variety of other foods; many eggplant dishes make up a basic part of vegetarian cuisine.

The elongated shape of hollowed-out zucchini and cucumbers makes them ideal for stuffing; variations on this theme are found in France, Mexico, Persia, India and China.

Some other choices of vegetables to stuff include onions, pumpkins, fennel and, of course, potatoes. The S.S. *France* was famous for its baked potatoes stuffed with Beluga caviar.

Roger Vergé, one of the three-star chefs of France, serves a selection of tiny stuffed vegetables from his native Provence. In this sun-drenched assortment he includes artichoke hearts filled with ham and spinach; small eggplants holding anchovies and olives; young onions stuffed with cheese and cream; small new potatoes with herbs and mushrooms; and little tomatoes stuffed with sausage meat.

Stuffed vegetables allow a cook great freedom and imagination. They range from simple home dishes to elegant extravaganzas for a feast.

STUFFED VEGE-TABLES

Stuffed vegetables make up a large and versatile category of dishes that range from simple, quickly prepared appetizers to rich and filling main

courses. Stuffing vegetables is an excellent way to highlight fresh vegetables when they are in season and it is a practical, attractive way to dress up leftovers and stretch luxurious ingredients.

Many vegetables are at their best served raw—small mushrooms, celery ribs, tomatoes, cucumbers, ripe avocados and even tender young zucchini can all be stuffed and served with no prior cooking.

Small stuffed tomatoes, mushroom caps, and cucumber cups and boats are delicious accompaniments for simply broiled and roasted meats or

chicken as well as good choices to serve on their own as a light luncheon dish.

Peppers, eggplant, squashes, potatoes and zucchini can all be stuffed and served as heartier fare as a main dish or to complement a chicken, chop or roast.

The tender leaves of cabbage, Swiss chard, lettuces and spinach can all be used to wrap around a tasty bit of stuffing, to be baked in a well-seasoned sauce. These make hearty and economical main dishes that are a delight to serve and eat. A whole stuffed cabbage is a real conversation stopper

Stuffing Cucumbers and Celery

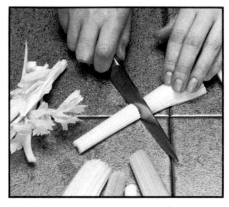

1 After trimming ends, leaves, and tough fibers, cut celery ribs into 3- to 4-inch lengths.

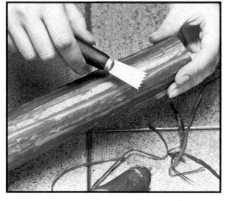

2 For raw cucumber cups, wash unpeeled cucumber. Score skin lengthwise with citrus zester or small sharp knife.

3 With small teaspoon scoop out seeds and all but ¼ inch of pulp from 1½- to 2-inch cucumber lengths.

4 Lightly salt cucumber cups and boats for baking. Drain on paper towels for 30 minutes. Rinse and blot dry.

5 Mound filling into prepared celery or cucumber.

6 Bake cucumber boats in greased baking dish until softened and stuffing is heated through.

that's fun to make and good to eat. For something more exotic, bring a Mediterranean accent to your table with stuffed grape leaves.

There are a number of ways stuffed vegetables can be prepared. It is important to select unblemished vegetables that are sufficiently large and appropriately shaped for your purpose. The leaves, the skins, the shells should all be firm enough to hold a filling. Some vegetables must be cut, cored or hollowed out before they can be stuffed. A small sharp paring knife is essential; a vegetable peeler and a melon-ball cutter are also useful tools to have

on hand. Certain vegetables may be blanched, or salted and drained, before stuffing.

Stuffed vegetables can be baked slowly in the oven or simmered gently on top of the stove. Select a heavy-bottomed casserole that has a tight-fitting lid and is just large enough to hold the vegetables in a single layer.

When baking stuffed vegetables, a small quantity of liquid—wine, stock or sauce—can be added to the baking dish to provide moisture and additional flavor. As long as the cooking pan is well oiled or buttered, however, the extra liquid is not essential.

Raw Vegetables

Avocado. Avocados must be ripe but not mushy, soft or blemished. Cut avocado into halves, remove pit, and sprinkle flesh with lemon or lime juice. Serve as a light lunch or first course.

Celery. Trim celery ribs and peel off any tough or discolored outer fibers. Cut into 3-inch lengths. Serve as an appetizer or part of a cocktail buffet.

Cucumber. Select firm young cucumbers that are not too big. If you can find them with the skins unwaxed, then leave skins on; otherwise peel

Stuffing Tomatoes

1 Slice off tops of tomatoes at stem end, or cut into halves through stem end, using a zigzag pattern if serving raw.

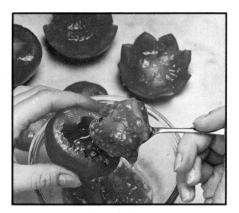

2 Scoop out pulp and seeds with small teaspoon, leaving about ½-inch layer of pulp inside; do not break the skin.

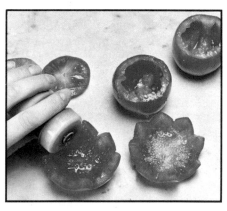

3 Sprinkle cut surfaces of tomato with salt; drain.

4 While tomatoes are draining, prepare ingredients for stuffing and cook if necessary.

5 To serve raw, fill tomato with prepared stuffing. Garnish and serve.

6 To cook, pour water to depth of ¼ inch into a greased baking dish containing stuffed tomatoes.

56

them. Cut each cucumber into 1½- to 2-inch lengths. Stand them on end and scoop out the seeds to make a hollow for the filling. Serve as an appetizer or part of a cocktail buffet.

Endive. Discard any bruised or discolored outer leaves. Gently remove or cut away each leaf until you reach the heart. This can be chopped and added to the filling of your choice. Serve as an appetizer or part of a cocktail buffet.

Mushrooms. Select small, perfectly shaped white mushrooms. Remove stems and reserve them for another use. Wipe caps clean and sprinkle with a little lemon juice to keep them from discoloring. They are ready for filling just as they are, or they may be marinated for up to 3 hours in vinaigrette dressing. Serve as an appetizer or part of a cocktail buffet.

Tomatoes. Use only flavorful tomatoes that have ripened on the vine. They should be ripe but firm, without any soft spots or blemishes. Cut away the stem end, removing approximately one third of the tomato. Cut zigzag patterns if you wish. Scoop out the seeds and pulp and place tomatoes upside down on a rack to drain. You can also sprinkle the inside with a little salt first to draw out excess liquid. Drain for about 30 minutes. Serve on a bed of lettuce as a light lunch or a first course.

Zucchini. Very young zucchini, not longer than 3 to 4 inches, are excellent uncooked and stuffed. Scrub under running water, trim off the ends and cut lengthwise into halves. Scoop out some of the flesh to make a hollow boat. Or prepare them in the same way as cucumbers. Serve as an appetizer or part of a cocktail buffet.

Fillings for Raw Vegetables

Choose from a wide variety of fillings for raw vegetables; you can easily invent others.

Soft creamy cheeses provide an elegant, smooth contrast to the crispy texture of raw vegetables. There are some good prepared cheeses seasoned with herbs, garlic and spices, or you can prepare your own. Cream

Preparing Vegetables for Stuffing

1 Slice squash lengthwise. Scoop out seeds and pulp from base and lid, leaving ½-inch border of pulp.

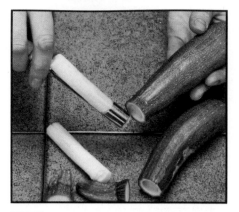

1 Core out center (seeds and pulp) of medium zucchini with apple corer. Cut ½-inch lengths from removed core to serve as plugs.

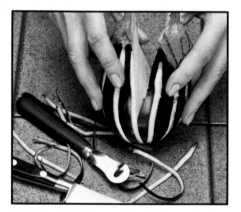

OR Split eggplant lengthwise through stem to within 1 inch from bottom. Remove alternating strips of peel.

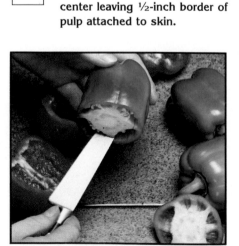

OR Cut stem end from eggplant; reserve for lid. Cut out large seeded center leaving ½-inch border of pulp attached to skin.

4 After rinsing salted shells or pulp under cold running water, pat dry with paper towels.

1 Remove stem end from bell peppers. Remove seeds and ribs from inside pepper. Rinse thoroughly to remove all seeds.

OR Zucchini can also be halved lengthwise for stuffing. Scoop out seeds and pulp, leaving ¼-inch border of pulp next to skin.	**1** To stuff eggplant halves, first cut out seeded center portion with knife, then scoop out all but ½ inch of pulp with teaspoon.

2 Sprinkle hollowed-out squash, zucchini or eggplant shells lightly with salt. Drain cut side down on paper towels for 30 minutes.	**3** If using removed pulp in stuffing, place in colander and sprinkle lightly with salt. Allow to drain for 30 minutes.

2 Blanch pepper in plenty of boiling water for 1 minute. Rinse blanched peppers in colander under cold running water.	**1** Cut thin slice from top of blanched onion and ease out the center, leaving ½-inch-thick shell for stuffing.

cheese, cottage cheese, even sour cream can be turned into delicious, zesty fillings. Add minced fresh herbs such as parsley, tarragon or dill. Add snips of chives, chopped scallions, garlic, if you wish. White pepper, cayenne, Tabasco and lemon juice can add a little zest.

Smooth liver pâté, ham spread, or other types of pâté make luxurious fillings.

Minced hard-cooked eggs, bound with well-seasoned mayonnaise; homemade potato salad, rice salad, or any other type of salad made with grains can be used.

Almost all seafood salads—crab meat, shrimps, lobster, salmon and tuna make good fillings for raw vegetables.

Spicy puréed lentils, chick-peas or other legumes are very good.

Large Fleshy Vegetables

Artichoke. A most attractive vegetable that seems designed for stuffing, either in between the leaves or in the cup-shaped bottom alone. The stuffed bottoms are prepared for many classic garnishes.

Artichokes may be precooked, cooled and then stuffed (see the directions for Artichokes Stuffed with Seafood Salad), or they may be stuffed and cooked together with the filling.

Prepare the artichokes as described in Steps 1 and 2, and reserve the stems. Soak artichokes and stems in a bowl of cold water to which salt and lemon juice have been added for 30 minutes.

Remove artichokes and drain them. They are now ready to be stuffed and braised. The stems may be peeled, diced, and added to the stuffing.

Artichoke bottoms make succulent containers for a variety of savory fillings. Trim and poach the bottoms, then stuff and bake them as you would stuffed mushroom caps.

To serve. Stuffed artichokes can be served hot from oven or broiler or at room temperature. Depending on the richness of the stuffing, they make an attractive first course to a meal, or they can serve as luncheon main dish or even a light supper. They are also used as a garnish, as in Tournedos Henri IV.

Cucumber. Although cucumbers are almost always served raw to take advantage of their crisp, fresh taste, they are delicious when stuffed and baked or braised.

Select firm, plump, large cucumbers. Peel them if the skin has been waxed, otherwise wash and score the skin as shown in the photograph. Cut cucumber lengthwise into halves, then scoop out the seeds and discard them. Sprinkle the hollowed cucumber boats with salt and let them drain hollowed side down on paper towels for 30 minutes and bake in a well-greased casserole at 350°F until the cucumber is just tender and stuffing is heated through, 15 to 20 minutes. Alternatively, braise them in a little stock in a covered casserole on top of the stove, for about 20 minutes.

To serve. Stuffed cucumber boats will dress up almost any simple main-course dish. Serve them with chicken, pork, veal, beef, or any simply prepared fish, such as poached salmon. When stuffed with a seafood salad, they make a handsome first course.

Eggplant. Choose shiny, smooth-skinned eggplants that are well shaped and not too large. During the season you may find some tiny, baby eggplants only 2½ to 3 inches long; these can be particularly delectable.

Eggplants can be prepared for stuffing in a number of ways, but they should never have their beautiful purple skin removed. To make hollow boats: Cut off the stem and cut the eggplant lengthwise into halves. Scoop out the pulp, but leave at least ½ inch to make the shell. Reserve the pulp.

For eggplants that are short and rounded: Cut off the stem end but leave the eggplant whole. Scoop out interior pulp to form a bowl. You may wish to use the cut-off stem end to make a cap or cover for the stuffed eggplant. Reserve the pulp.

Or make lengthwise slits from end to end, leaving 1 inch across the bottom uncut to keep the slices hinged. Spoon stuffing into the gaps between the slices.

Regardless of the preparation, sprinkle the eggplant shells and the reserved pulp with salt. Let drain for 30 minutes, rinse with cold water, and pat dry. Chop the reserved eggplant pulp and use it in stuffing if desired.

To serve. Depending on the ingredients used for stuffing and the size of the eggplant you have chosen, there are many ways eggplants can be served. When stuffed with meat and grains, stuffed eggplants make a hearty, satisfying main-course dish. They can accompany a chicken or a roast. Small stuffed eggplants can be allowed to cool, to be served as appetizers on their own or as part of a cocktail buffet.

Fennel. A most delicious vegetable with a slight hint of sweetness in its anise-scented flesh. Unfortunately, it is a vegetable that is all too much ignored.

Trim the fennel bulbs but leave enough of the root end to hold the bulb together. Reserve the leaves and ribs for another use. Blanch fennel bulbs in salted water for 10 minutes. Drain and let cool. Cut fennel bulb lengthwise into halves and remove enough center layers and core to make a hollow boat. Do not discard these inner layers. They should be diced and added to the stuffing.

Stuff fennel boats and bake them with a little chicken stock in a covered baking dish at 350°F for 30 minutes.

To serve. Depending on the richness of the stuffing, serve the stuffed fennel to complement a roasted chicken, capon or turkey. Or serve them on their own for lunch or a light supper.

Mushrooms. Large, meaty mushroom caps make ideal little saucers to heap with stuffing and bake or braise in a little stock.

Select the largest mushrooms you can find, eliminating any bruised or broken ones. Remove the stems carefully to avoid any damage to the cap and put stems aside for later use. Use a dampened soft dishcloth or paper towel to wipe the caps clean. Brush the outside of the mushroom caps with melted butter or vegetable oil and they are ready to be stuffed with your choice of filling. Arrange them in a shallow, ovenproof pan and bake at 350°F until mushrooms are soft and the filling is lightly browned. Or add a little liquid—stock or white wine—cover the pan, and braise them in the oven or on top of the stove for about 20 minutes, until they are done.

To serve. Stuffed mushrooms may be served hot or cooled to room temperature. They can accompany a simple roast or steak. Or serve them as an appetizer or first course.

Onions. Onions are a perfect example of how a plain vegetable can be transformed into something exotic by the addition of a stuffing.

Select the firmest, largest onions you can find. Onions ideal for stuffing should measure 3½ to 4 inches across the middle. Inspect each onion to make sure that it has perfect, shiny, tight-fitting skin and that there are no soft spots hidden underneath.

Peel them and cut away a ½-inch slice from the top. Scoop out the center pulp to make a hollow, but leave at least a ½-inch wall around the sides and bottom. Reserve the scooped-out onion; chop it to fine pieces and add it to the stuffing.

Blanch the hollowed onions in boiling water for 3 to 5 minutes, until they are barely tender but still firm. Or blanch whole onions before scooping out the centers. Drain them upside down on paper towels. They are now ready to be filled and baked with broth or wine at 350°F for 40 to 50 minutes.

To serve. Serve them with any roasted poultry, beef or pork.

Peppers. Almost every variety of pepper is suitable for stuffing. For charm, simplicity and ease of preparation, however, bell peppers are the best. Choose either red or green or the occasionally available yellow peppers. If you are preparing them in any quantity, choose several of each color to make a colorful display. Try to select peppers that are all of the same size.

Prepare small peppers by slicing off the stem end and setting it aside to use it later as a lid. Remove the seeds and ribs from the interior and rinse the hollowed peppers under cold running water.

Large peppers can be cut lengthwise into halves, leaving half of the stem attached to each piece to make a natural handle. Remove the seeds and ribs and rinse.

The hollowed peppers may be blanched in boiling water for 3 to 5 minutes. Remove peppers and drain on paper towels. Blanching insures that the peppers will be cooked soft in the final baking. If you prefer them to retain a crunch, omit the blanching.

Stuff peppers with the filling of your choice. If the stuffing ingredients have been precooked, bake them in a well-greased ovenproof pan at 350°F for 25 to 30 minutes. If the stuffing ingredients are raw, allow longer, according to the ingredients.

To serve. Most often, stuffed peppers make a satisfying main dish on their own. There is room for improvisation, however, as they are also delicious served at room temperature, as part of a buffet, or even as a side dish to a roast.

Potatoes. The premium choice is the large Idaho or Russet potato, but all potatoes bake extremely well.

Select well-shaped potatoes without blemishes or bruises, which have not begun to sprout. Scrub the potatoes with a brush and dry them well.

Rub skins with vegetable oil if you want softer skins. Without the oil the skins retain a firmer, crisper texture.

Bake potatoes in the oven at 400°F for 40 to 50 minutes; the time is

Stuffing Baked Potatoes

1 Cut deep cross in top of potato to open. Top with sour cream or yogurt and snipped fresh chives.

1 Combine about 1 cup sweet corn kernels, 2 tablespoons finely chopped walnuts and butter with the pulp from 4 baked potatoes.

1 Sauté 4 bacon slices, diced, ½ cup sliced mushrooms and 1 minced small onion for 4 minutes. Mix with potato pulp. Bake.

1 Halve a baked potato and mash the pulp with butter and seasoning. Break egg into each half and bake at 350°F for 20 minutes.

1 Mix 2 egg yolks, 8 chopped anchovy fillets, butter, seasonings with pulp of 4 potatoes. Fold in 2 beaten egg whites. Bake.

1 Combine pulp from 4 potatoes, ¼ cup flaked smoked fish, 2 tablespoons chopped parsley, butter and pinch of cayenne. Bake.

approximate and depends on size of the potatoes. To see if they are done, pierce a potato with a sharp knife; if the pulp resists, then bake them a little longer.

Remove potatoes; halve or slash a crisscross pattern in each one. Potatoes are now ready to be stuffed in a variety of ways.

When tiny new potatoes are in season, prepare them for cooking as described above. Bake them for approximately 20 minutes. As soon as they are cool enough to handle, pinch them open and fill each one with a dollop of sour cream and top it off with caviar. These make a delectable, luxurious bite-size hors d'oeuvre.

To serve. Baked stuffed potatoes are so unfailingly popular and satisfying you can serve them any time at all. Have them for breakfast, lunch, brunch, cocktails, dinner or midnight snack. They go with almost every kind of dish, or can be served gloriously on their own.

Tomatoes. When fresh, vine-ripened tomatoes are at the height of their season and available in great abundance, stuffing and baking them provides variety and is a delicious way to use a surplus of this flavorful fruit.

Prepare the tomatoes as illustrated. Stuff with well-seasoned bread crumbs or any other filling of your choice. Place in a well-greased baking dish and bake at 350°F for 15 to 20 minutes; tomatoes should be tender and the filling heated through.

To serve. Stuffed baked tomatoes are classic accompaniments to broiled steaks, chops, and roasted leg of lamb. They are also delicious at room temperature as part of a buffet.

Zucchini and Other Summer Squashes. Select firm, well-shaped squashes and zucchini. In season there is a great range of sizes; select according to your need.

Zucchini and other summer squashes should not be peeled. Scrub under running water and dry. Cut them lengthwise into halves and scoop out seeds and, if the vegetables are very large, a little of the pulp.

Alternatively, slice off the stem end and use a spoon, butter knife or apple corer to scoop out seeds and pulp, boring a hole through the interior.

Or prepare hollowed-out rings by cutting the squash crosswise into 2-inch lengths; scoop out seeds to make small hollow cups.

Stuff and bake them as for cucumbers.

To serve. Serve hot with main-course dishes, or tepid, as part of a buffet.

Cooking Stuffed Vegetables

1 Choose an appropriate-size dish. Coat it lightly with oil, if no liquid is to be used.

2 Spoon stuffing into vegetable, packing tightly if the stuffing is cooked, loosely if raw.

3 Arrange the vegetables carefully in the dish, putting them close together.

4 If using liquid, pour it around vegetables; cover. Cook in moderate oven or simmer on top of stove, according to recipe.

Fillings for Large Fleshy Vegetables

The list of possible fillings for vegetables is enormous; there is great scope for creativity and experimentation. The fillings can be lavish or economical.

Fillings may include bread crumbs, croutons, rice or other grains, pasta, beans. If meat is included, it is usually precooked or briefly sautéed on top of the stove.

Cooked fillings are generally prepared in advance, except when cheese

Stuffing and Cooking a Whole Cabbage

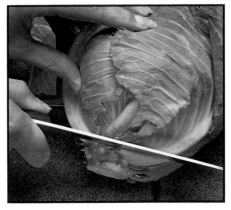

1 Thoroughly wash cabbage. Trim off all the tough outer leaves and the stalk.

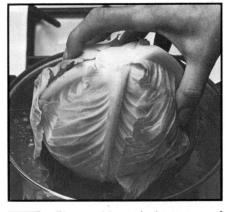

2 Place cabbage in large pan of boiling salted water; blanch for 4 minutes. Drain, rinse and pat dry.

3 Place the whole cabbage on the board and carefully open out the leaves without detaching them.

4 To stuff between the leaves, carefully spread each leaf with some of the stuffing.

OR Remove cabbage heart, chop and add it to stuffing if wished, then spoon stuffing into the cavity.

5 Gently push the cabbage into its original shape and tie up with string or muslin.

6 Put cabbage in casserole lined with trimmings, onion, garlic, bay leaf, thyme and seasoning.

7 Simmer, covered, for about 3 hours in moderate oven or on top of stove.

8 Lift out the cabbage on to a board. Remove string or muslin and arrange the cabbage on a dish.

and minced raw vegetables form the base of the stuffing.

Cooked fish and poultry, sautéed chicken livers, chopped bacon, minced ham, cooked vegetables and grated cheese can all be used to advantage.

An equal quantity of cooked rice and minced lamb or beef is a commonly used mixture. If you want to be really economical, you can leave out the meat altogether. Make a tasty vegetarian mixture with an all-rice stuffing or a rice and split-pea or chick-pea stuffing, or a rice and vegetable stuffing such as onions, tomatoes, mushrooms, etc.

All these stuffings, and particularly the meatless ones, need careful flavoring with herbs and spices. Chopped parsley is excellent and can be used lavishly; chopped fresh mint is also good as are thyme, basil, orégano and marjoram.

Curry powder or paste, cinnamon, allspice, cuminseed and coriander are all useful additions. Most stuffings are improved by the addition of a chopped and fried onion, while a skinned and chopped tomato adds moisture as well as flavor.

Pine nuts, chopped almonds, cashews and walnuts all make good additions, providing food value as well as flavor and texture. Small quantities of dried fruits such as currants, raisins and chopped dried apricots are also good.

Sometimes vegetables alone can be used to make the stuffing; a mixture of chopped tomatoes, onions and parsley, fried in oil with garlic is a classic combination. If bread crumbs are added as well, this makes a tasty stuffing.

Leafy Vegetables

Cabbage. Whole cabbage for stuffing should be of good shape, hearty but not too firmly packed; you need to be able to separate the leaves in order to put in the stuffing. Savoy cabbages are ideal. Wash the cabbage thoroughly under cold running water. Trim off tough outer leaves and stem.

Prepare the cabbage for stuffing by blanching it. Bring a large pan half full of water to the boil, plunge in the cabbage, stem end up, bring back to the boil and cook uncovered for 4 minutes. Drain and rinse under cold water. Pat dry with kitchen paper.

Cabbage leaves are easier to prepare and stuff than a whole cabbage. The leaves should be fairly large but tender. Again, Savoy and other loose-leaved cabbages are excellent. Wash the leaves, cut off the stems level with the base of the leaf and, if the stem is very tough, cut away a triangle of the rib from the leaf.

Blanch the leaves in boiling water for 4 minutes, drain, run under cold water, and pat dry.

Grape Leaves. Grape leaves are often not obtainable fresh. When they are, wash and blanch as for cabbage leaves. Canned or bottled grape leaves can be used instead of fresh and are very good. Take the leaves out of can or jar and rinse them under running water to remove brine, then blanch for 1 minute; drain, rinse, and pat dry.

Lettuce. Large-leaved lettuces make excellent wrappers to stuff. Plunge the entire head of lettuce into boiling water for 2 minutes to tenderize the leaves. Drain, rinse, and pat dry.

Spinach. Spinach leaves should be large and well shaped. Wash very carefully and cut the stem level with the leaf. Blanch as for cabbage, but for 2 or 3 minutes only; the leaves should be soft and pliable so they will roll round the stuffing easily. Rinse and pat dry.

Swiss Chard. Swiss chard leaves can also be stuffed. Prepare in the same way as cabbage leaves.

Fillings for Leafy Vegetables

Many of the fillings suggested for large fleshy vegetables can also be used to stuff leafy vegetables.

Mixtures of rice and meat, or rice and beans, are delicious wrapped in cabbage, spinach or grape leaves. The rice and meat may be used raw; dried beans should be precooked.

Whole cooked chestnuts or well-seasoned chestnut purée mixed with chopped onions and celery make excellent stuffings for cabbage leaves.

The filling for a whole cabbage may be put in raw if the cabbage is to be stuffed between the leaves. However, if you intend to remove the heart from the cabbage and stuff the cavity, the filling must be precooked. Fillings can be a mixture of meat and vegetables with rice. Fried onion, chopped tomato, celery, peppers and mushrooms can be added, with garlic, herbs and spices to taste.

Chopped pineapple, apples and raisins can be included to add a touch of sweetness.

Stuffing Leafy Vegetables

Roll tender spinach or cabbage leaves around a savory filling (or stuff a whole cabbage), bake in a flavorful sauce, and the result is an economical dish which uses only a small amount of meat, or even cooked leftovers.

Since these dishes require slow cooking, use a heavy casserole with a tight-fitting lid. Oil the bottom of the casserole and line with a layer of sliced peeled tomatoes, chopped carrot and onion, or some of the unstuffed leaves to prevent sticking.

To stuff leaves, first blanch them. Drain, dry, and arrange smooth side down on a work surface. Place 2 to 3 teaspoons of filling just below the center of the leaf, more for a large cabbage leaf. Fold the stem end over the stuffing, fold over the two sides, and roll into a compact cylinder. Place the stuffed leaves, seam side down, side by side in the lined casserole. When the bottom is covered, start another layer on top. Add about 2 tablespoons of oil, and enough stock, tomato juice, wine or other liquid to reach a depth of 1 inch.

Cook stuffed leaves, covered, over low heat or in a preheated 300° to 325°F oven for 30 to 60 minutes, or until stuffing is cooked. A stuffed whole cabbage, whether stuffed in the center or between the leaves, will take between 2 and 3 hours, depending on the stuffing.

Stuffed Vegetable Leaves

1 Wash leaves in large bowl or sink of lukewarm water to remove sand and grit.

2 Trim leaf stem even with base of leaf. Cut out any thick tough rib from center of leaf.

3 After draining and blanching leaves, spread them out on flat surface, smooth side down. Blot dry with paper towels.

4 Line bottom of greased casserole with blanched leaves. Sliced tomatoes or chopped carrots and onions can also be used.

5 Place filling near stem end just below center of leaf.

6 Fold stem end of leaf over to cover filling. Then fold in both sides of leaf to enclose filling completely.

7 Roll leaf and filling into a tight cylinder, pressing gently as you work to keep roll compact.

8 Arrange leaf rolls, seam side down, snugly in bottom of casserole. Stack one layer on top of another until all rolls are used.

9 Pour enough liquid into casserole to cover bottom by about 1 inch.

Artichokes Stuffed with Seafood Salad

6 portions

6 globe artichokes
1 lemon, cut up
    lemon juice or vinegar
    salt
2 tablespoons snipped chives
2 tablespoons minced
     parsley
6 canned anchovy fillets
1 teaspoon capers
½ pound white fish, cooked
½ pound shrimps, cooked
     and peeled, diced if large
¾ cup Mayonnaise (see
     Index)
⅛ teaspoon paprika
     freshly ground pepper

1 Cut off artichoke stems and tough outer leaves. Rinse, shake dry, and rub cut parts with lemon.

2 Trim tips of leaves with scissors. Fan open outer leaves, pull out inner leaves and scrape away hairy choke.

• The stem of the artichoke is meaty and delicious, just like the heart. Reserve the cut-off stems, peel them with a sharp knife or vegetable peeler, and cook along with artichokes until they are just tender. Eat them separately or chop them and add to the stuffing.

• Good choices for the fish are cod, halibut, bass, flounder and monkfish. Don't hesitate to use leftover fish that has been poached or broiled.

• Other seafood possibilities include cooked crab meat, lobster, scallops, even mussels.

• Vary the seasonings by adding curry powder, tarragon, fresh dill, cayenne or basil.

• Dilute the mayonnaise with yogurt for a lighter dressing.

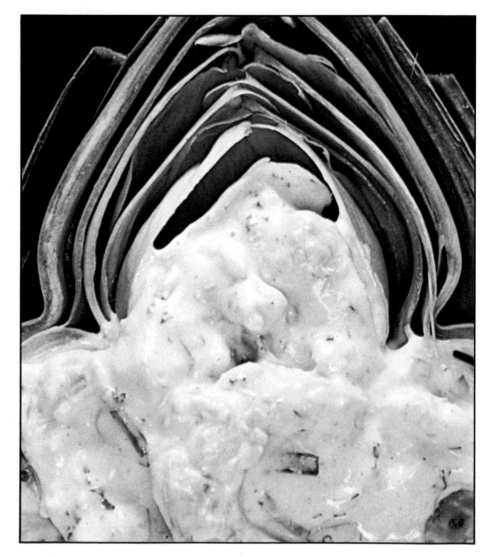

3 Plunge upside down in a large pan of boiling water. Add a little lemon juice or vinegar and salt.

4 Cook for 15 to 40 minutes, depending on size. Turn occasionally. Leaves pull away easily when the artichoke is cooked.

5 Squeeze cooked artichokes gently to press out water. Drain upside down and leave until cold.

6 Mix chives and parsley. Drain and chop anchovies and capers.

7 Turn the fish into a bowl and separate into coarse flakes with a fork. Add peeled shrimps.

8 Add herbs, capers and anchovies. Mix lemon juice with mayonnaise and stir into fish. Season.

9 Open artichokes a little and carefully spoon some of the stuffing into the center of each.

10 To eat, use fingers to pull off a leaf. Dip into the stuffing and scrape fleshy base between teeth.

11 When all outer leaves are eaten, use knife and fork to cut artichoke bottom into chunks.

Peppers Stuffed with Tomatoes and Tuna

4 portions

4	large red, green or yellow bell peppers	¼	teaspoon black pepper
1	medium-size onion	12	ounces canned water-packed tuna
2	garlic cloves	4	anchovy fillets
4	tablespoons olive oil	6	pitted black olives
3½	cups canned peeled tomatoes	1	tablespoon minced fresh parsley
1	tablespoon tomato purée	2	teaspoons capers
½	teaspoon dried basil	1	ounce Parmesan cheese, grated (¼ cup)
½	teaspoon dried orégano		
½	teaspoon salt		

With a sharp knife cut off 1 inch from the stem end of each pepper. Remove and discard the seeds and ribs. Remove stems from the sliced tops and chop the rest of the tops. Peel and slice the onion. Peel and crush the garlic.

In a large frying pan, heat 2 tablespoons of the oil over moderate heat. When oil is hot, add the onion, garlic and pepper dice and sauté, stirring occasionally, for 5 to 7 minutes, until onion is soft and translucent but not brown. Add tomatoes with the juice from the can, the tomato purée, basil, orégano, salt and pepper. Cover the pan and cook, stirring occasionally, for 20 to 30 minutes, or until the mixture is thick. Drain and flake the tuna. Chop the anchovy fillets and olives. Stir tuna and anchovies into the tomato mixture, along with the parsley, olives and capers, and cook for 5 minutes longer.

Preheat oven to 325°F. Remove the frying pan from heat and spoon the tomato and tuna mixture into the peppers, filling them to within ½ inch of the top. With a pastry brush, coat a baking pan with 1 tablespoon of the remaining oil. Place peppers in the baking pan and put it in the oven. Bake the peppers for 45 minutes, basting occasionally with remaining oil. After 45 minutes, sprinkle the tops of the peppers with the grated cheese and bake for 15 minutes longer, until the cheese is browned and bubbly.

Remove peppers from the oven and serve immediately.

Cabbage with Curried Cheese Stuffing

4 to 6 portions

1 head of green cabbage, 2 pounds
8 ounces yellow onions
1 red apple, Winesap or Delicious
6 ounces Cheddar cheese, grated (1½ cups)
2 tablespoons vegetable oil

1 tablespoon curry powder
1 tablespoon tomato purée
¼ cup uncooked long-grain rice
1 large egg
salt and pepper
1 cup chicken stock

Bring a large pan of salted water (1 teaspoon salt for 4 cups water) to a boil. Wash and trim the cabbage, cutting out the core. Blanch the whole head, stem end uppermost, for 4 minutes. Drain and pat dry with paper towels. Peel and mince the onions and the apple. Heat the oil in a saucepan; sauté onions and apple in the hot oil over moderate heat for 10 minutes. Add the curry powder and cook for 2 minutes longer, stirring all the while. Remove pan from heat and stir in cheese, tomato purée, rice, egg, and salt and pepper to taste. Mix well.

Carefully stuff the cabbage, spreading the filling between the leaves but keeping the head together. Wrap the cabbage in a double layer of cheesecloth and tie; place the bundle in a deep heavy casserole.

Pour the stock into the pan around the cabbage and set the saucepan over low heat. Cover and cook gently for about 3 hours, until the stuffing is cooked and the cabbage tender. If in doubt, test with a long thin skewer. Cut the cabbage head into wedges to serve.

Cabbage Leaves with Chicken-Liver Stuffing

6 portions

1 head of Savoy cabbage, 2 pounds
vegetable oil for baking dish
1 medium-size onion
1 celery rib
1 garlic clove
12 ounces fresh chicken livers

2 tablespoons butter
salt
4 ounces sausage meat
3 tablespoons tomato purée
1 teaspoon dried thyme
freshly ground black pepper
1 cup chicken stock

Cut out the cabbage core to make it easy to separate the leaves. Keep the largest outer leaves to one side. Wash the reserved outer leaves and all the rest. Cut out the thickest part of the rib in the center of each leaf to flatten the leaf. Bring a large pan of water to a boil and blanch the leaves for 4 minutes. Drain and rinse with cold water. Spread out the leaves, ribbed sides up, on a work surface and pat them dry with paper towels. Lightly oil a baking dish, 6- to 8-cup size. Line the dish with the reserved outer leaves of cabbage.

Prepare the stuffing: Peel and mince the onion. Wash, dry, and mince the celery. Peel and crush the garlic, or put it through a press. Rinse chicken livers in a sieve and trim off any green bits. Chop livers. Melt the butter in a skillet. Add the chicken livers, sprinkle them with salt, and sauté over moderate heat for 4 minutes. With a slotted spoon transfer livers to a medium-size bowl. Add onion, celery and garlic to the

skillet and cook until soft. With a fork, mash the chicken livers to a paste. Add to the liver paste the sautéed onion, celery and garlic, the sausage meat, tomato purée, thyme and black pepper to taste. Mix well.

Put about 1 tablespoon of the stuffing mixture on each cabbage leaf, placing it just above the center of the leaf. Turn the stem end over the stuffing, fold in both sides, then roll the leaf over to enclose the stuffing completely, making each leaf into a neat cylinder. Arrange the stuffed leaves, seam sides down, close together on the cabbage leaves in the baking dish. When the bottom of the dish is covered, make another layer on top. Pour in the stock. Put the dish over high heat for 3 minutes, cover it, then reduce heat and simmer the stuffed leaves for 50 minutes.

Take the stuffed leaves out with tongs or 2 spoons and arrange them on a warmed serving dish. Serve immediately.

Stuffed Arabian Eggplants

4 portions

4	eggplants, 10 to 12 ounces each	6	ounces ground cooked lamb or beef
	salt	½	teaspoon ground cuminseed
6	tablespoons uncooked rice	½	teaspoon ground coriander
½	cup raisins		salt and black pepper
2	ounces pine nuts	2	cups beef stock
2	large tomatoes	3	tablespoons chopped fresh parsley
1	medium-size onion		
1	tablespoon olive oil		

Wash eggplants and remove stems and leaves. Halve eggplants lengthwise and scoop out the pulp, leaving a shell about ¾-inch thick. Place pulp in a colander and sprinkle with salt. Salt the shells and place them upside down in a colander or on a rack to drain for 30 minutes.

Place rice in a saucepan and pour in ¾ cup water. Bring to a boil over high heat, stir once, cover, and simmer gently for about 15 minutes. Five minutes before the rice is done, stir in the raisins and pine nuts. If rice becomes dry before it is tender, add more water, 1 tablespoon at a time.

Blanch the tomatoes in boiling water for 1 minute; drain. Peel, halve and remove as many seeds as possible. Chop the pulp. Peel and mince the onion. Sauté onion in the oil over low heat. Rinse the eggplant pulp and shells in cold water. Pat shells dry and press the pulp to release as much water as possible. Chop the pulp.

Place ground lamb or beef in a large bowl and stir in the chopped eggplant, cooked rice and raisins, chopped tomatoes, sautéed onion, spices, and seasoning to taste. Mix well. Arrange the eggplant shells in a single layer in an oiled baking dish. Spoon in the stuffing, packing it loosely to allow for expansion during baking. If there is too much stuffing for the shells, bake it in a separate small casserole.

Pour enough of the stock into the dish to come halfway up the sides of the eggplants; use more if needed. Cover the dish. Simmer the stuffed eggplants on top of the stove for 45 minutes to 1 hour, until eggplants are tender and the stuffing cooked. Garnish with parsley before serving.

Belgian Endives Stuffed with Cheese and Nuts

20 appetizers

- 6 ounces cream cheese
- 6 tablespoons heavy cream
- ⅛ teaspoon cayenne pepper
- ¼ teaspoon salt
- ¼ teaspoon freshly ground white pepper
- ½ teaspoon prepared Dijon-style mustard
- 1 teaspoon Worcestershire sauce
- ½ cup chopped walnuts
- ½ cup chopped hazelnuts
- 20 large Belgian endive leaves

In a medium-size mixing bowl, mash cream cheese with a fork until soft and smooth. Add cream, cayenne, salt, pepper, mustard and Worcestershire sauce; beat well to blend ingredients thoroughly. Stir in walnuts and hazelnuts.

Wash and dry the endive leaves. Put 1 tablespoon of the cheese mixture, or a little more, on each endive leaf. Arrange stuffed leaves on a serving platter and chill for at least 30 minutes before serving as an appetizer or cocktail snack.

Dolmades

(Stuffed Grape Leaves)

In Greece stuffed grape-vine leaves are served cold as an hors d'oeuvre, garnished with lemon wedges, or hot, often with a selection of other vegetables with different stuffings.

4 to 6 portions as a main dish, 12 to 15 as an hors d'oeuvre

- 40 to 50 grape leaves
- 1 medium-size onion
- 4 tablespoons olive oil
- 6 tablespoons uncooked long-grain rice
- salt and black pepper
- 1 cup chicken stock
- 2 ounces pine nuts
- 2 ounces dried currants
- 1 lemon
- 1 cup tomato juice

If the grape leaves are fresh, blanch them in boiling salted water for 5 minutes. If the leaves are canned or packed in a jar, rinse them and blanch for 1 minute. Drain, rinse with very cold water, spread out on a work surface, and pat leaves dry with paper towels.

Peel and mince the onion. Heat 2 tablespoons of the oil in a saucepan and sauté the onion for 5 minutes. Add the rice, seasoning to taste and the stock. Cover and simmer until the rice is tender and the liquid absorbed.

Sauté the pine nuts in the rest of the oil over medium heat until lightly browned. Mix together the rice, pine nuts, currants and more seasoning if needed.

Put a teaspoon of the stuffing on the back of most of the grape leaves; leave a few unstuffed to line the baking dish. Roll up each stuffed leaf into a neat parcel. Line the baking dish with the unstuffed leaves and arrange the little parcels side by side in the dish. Squeeze the lemon and pour the juice over the parcels. Add tomato juice to the dish. Put a plate on top of the rolls to keep them in place and prevent unrolling during cooking. Cover the pan. Cook over high heat for 3 minutes, then reduce heat and simmer gently for about 50 minutes.

Variations: For *dolmades* with meat filling, add 8 ounces minced raw lamb to the sautéed onion and cook for 5 minutes. Add 1 tablespoon minced parsley and 2 teaspoons each of chopped fresh sage and mint. For *dolmades* with yogurt sauce, make either the basic recipe or the meat variation; omit tomato juice and substitute an equal volume of chicken stock. Stir 3 tablespoons plain yogurt into the strained sauce before serving.

Spinach Leaves with Mushroom Stuffing

4 portions

20	large spinach leaves
2	medium-size onions
8	ounces fresh mushrooms
1	garlic clove
3	tablespoons butter
1	large egg
1½	cups fresh white bread crumbs

	pinch of grated nutmeg
	salt and black pepper
	vegetable oil for baking dish
1	cup chicken stock
1	egg yolk
½	lemon

Bring a large pan of salted water (1 teaspoon salt for 4 cups water) to a boil. Wash the spinach leaves and trim the stems level with the leaves. Plunge spinach into the boiling water and blanch for 2 minutes. Drain, rinse with ice water, and drain again. Carefully separate the leaves and arrange them on a work surface. Pat leaves dry with paper towels. Set 4 leaves aside to line the baking dish.

Prepare the stuffing: Peel and mince the onions. Wipe the mushrooms with a damp cloth, trim base of the stems, and slice caps and stems. Peel garlic and put through a press into the onions. Melt the butter in a saucepan and add the onions and garlic. Sauté over low heat until onions are soft. Add the mushrooms and continue cooking until mushrooms are done. Beat the whole egg in a bowl. Remove the pan of onions and mushrooms from the heat and stir the mixture into the beaten egg. Add the bread crumbs, nutmeg, and salt and pepper to taste.

Put 1 tablespoon of the stuffing on each spinach leaf and roll up carefully. Lightly oil a shallow baking dish. Place the reserved spinach leaves in the dish and arrange the stuffed leaves on top, in a single layer. Pour in the stock, bring to a boil, and boil for 3 minutes. Reduce the heat, cover the dish, and simmer for 30 minutes.

Beat the extra egg yolk and the lemon juice together in a cup. Lift out the cooked spinach rolls and place them on a warmed serving dish. Strain the cooking liquid into a small saucepan and bring to a boil. Add a few spoonfuls of the hot liquid to the egg mixture, stirring all the while. Reduce heat under the saucepan to moderate and pour in the egg and lemon mixture, stirring, and keep over heat until the sauce is thickened. Do not boil or it will curdle. Serve the sauce separately to accompany the stuffed spinach leaves.

Herb-Stuffed Pattypan Squash

6 portions

6	white pattypan squashes, about 4 ounces each		3	tablespoons snipped fresh chives
1	small onion		½	teaspoon crushed dried rosemary
2	to 3 tablespoons vegetable oil		1	tablespoon lemon juice
½	cup chopped walnuts		1½	cups fresh white bread crumbs
4	tablespoons chopped fresh parsley		2	tablespoons butter, cold

Wash squashes; cut out the stems. With a melon-ball cutter, scoop out the entire seed portion of each squash and discard it. Blanch the squashes in boiling water for 5 minutes. Drain, rinse with cold water, and drain again, upside down.

Peel and mince the onion. Heat 1 tablespoon of the oil in a skillet and sauté the onion until tender, but not browned. Stir in walnuts and sauté and stir until walnuts are crisp on the edges; if the pan becomes dry, add a little more of the oil. Stir in all the herbs, mixing them in well, and cook for 1 minute longer. Remove pan from heat and stir in lemon juice and 1 cup of the bread crumbs. Let the stuffing cool for 10 minutes.

Preheat oven to 350°F. Spoon the filling into the squashes, pressing it in rather firmly. Sprinkle the rest of the bread crumbs over the filling and the tops of the little squashes. Cut the butter into bits no larger than a lentil and divide the bits among the squashes. Brush a large baking pan, or 2 smaller pans, with remaining vegetable oil and set the squashes on it. Bake in the preheated oven for about 45 minutes, until the crumb topping is brown and crisp and the squashes tender; test with a thin skewer to be sure.

Stuffed Onions with Cheesy Topping

4 portions

4	large Spanish onions			salt and black pepper
8	teaspoons vegetable oil		3	ounces shelled hazelnuts
1	small green pepper		¼	cup rolled oats
4	ounces plum tomatoes		2	ounces Parmesan cheese, grated (¼ cup)
1	garlic clove		½	cup light cream
1	teaspoon dried thyme			

Bring a large pan of salted water (1 teaspoon salt to 4 cups water) to a boil. Peel the onions and blanch them in the boiling water for 4 minutes. Drain and rinse under very cold water. Cut a slice from the top of each onion. Using a melon-ball scoop, carefully ease out the center of each onion to make a hollow, leaving a shell at least ½-inch thick; if necessary to make the shell thicker, do so, lest they fall apart in baking.

Preheat oven to 350°F. Coat a deep baking dish lightly with about 2 teaspoons of the oil. Place the onions in the dish. Wash the pepper, discard stem, seeds and ribs, and rinse it out. Chop the pepper and half of the onion scooped from the shells. Heat remaining oil in a saucepan, add chopped onion and green pepper, and cook over moderate heat until vegetables are tender and onions golden.

Pour boiling water over the tomatoes; leave for 1 minute. Peel tomatoes, halve and discard as many seeds as possible. Chop the pulp. Add tomatoes to the saucepan and cook until most of the liquid has evaporated. Peel the garlic and put through a press into the pan, along with the thyme and salt and pepper to taste. Divide the stuffing among the onions, heaping it up in the center.

Crush hazelnuts and combine with oats, grated cheese and light cream. Season the mixture to taste, then spoon it evenly over the onions. Cover the dish, making sure the lid does not touch the topping. Bake for 1½ hours, until onions are soft and the topping browned.

Peppers Stuffed with Lamb and Rice

4 portions

4	large red or green bell peppers	1	teaspoon salt
1	small onion	½	teaspoon black pepper
1	garlic clove	1	teaspoon coriander seeds
4	teaspoons vegetable oil	2	cups cooked long-grain rice
8	ounces ground cooked lamb	1	teaspoon chopped mint leaves, or ½ teaspoon dried
1¾	cups canned peeled tomatoes		

With a sharp knife slice off 1 inch from the stem end of each pepper. Remove and discard seeds and ribs. Rinse the peppers.

Preheat oven to 375°F. Peel and chop onion. Peel garlic and put through a press. In a medium-size saucepan, heat 3 teaspoons of the oil over moderate heat. When oil is hot, add onion and garlic and sauté, stirring occasionally, for 5 to 7 minutes, until onion is soft and translucent but not brown. Add the ground lamb and cook, stirring constantly, for 6 to 8 minutes, until lamb is well browned. Add tomatoes with the juice from the can, the salt, pepper, and crushed coriander seeds. Cover the pan, reduce heat to low, and simmer for 30 minutes. Add the rice and mint and cook, still stirring, for 5 minutes longer. Remove pan from heat.

Using a pastry brush, coat a medium-size baking pan with remaining oil. Spoon equal amounts of the lamb mixture into each pepper. Stand the peppers upright in the baking dish and place the dish in the center of the oven. Bake for 40 minutes, or until the peppers are tender.

Remove peppers from the oven and serve immediately. A green salad is an excellent accompaniment.

Dolma

(Stuffed Eggplants, Zucchini and Tomatoes)

Dolma is a Middle Eastern dish of mixed vegetables stuffed with lamb and rice. Serve for a first course, or for a main dish accompanied with a green salad.

6 portions

3	small eggplants, each about 10 ounces	6	tablespoons cooked rice
2	teaspoons salt	3	tablespoons chopped fresh parsley
6	zucchini, each about 6 ounces	2	tablespoons coriander seeds, crushed
6	tomatoes, each about 6 ounces	½	teaspoon ground cuminseed
1	large onion	1	teaspoon ground turmeric
2	garlic cloves	½	teaspoon black pepper
2	tablespoons olive oil	2	large eggs
1½	pounds raw lamb, ground	2	tablespoons melted butter

Wash eggplants and halve them lengthwise. Sprinkle the cut sides with 1 teaspoon salt and put them upside down in a colander to drain for 30 minutes.

Wash zucchini and dry thoroughly with paper towels. Cut off about ½ inch from each end of the zucchini. With an apple corer, carefully scoop out the centers. Cut the tops off the tomatoes and hollow out the centers; keep the tops; set tomato shells upside down to drain. Rinse the eggplants and pat dry. With a melon-ball scoop cut out the centers, leaving a shell about ¾-inch thick. All these portions scooped out from the vegetables are not used in the recipe. They may be refrigerated for another use (soup, stew, etc.).

Preheat oven to 350°F. Peel and mince onion. Peel garlic and put through a press into the onion. Heat the oil in a large frying pan over moderate heat. When oil is hot, add onion and garlic and sauté for 8 minutes, until onion is light brown. Stir in the lamb and cook, stirring occasionally, for 10 minutes, until the meat has lost all its pinkness. Remove pan from heat and turn the mixture into a large mixing bowl.

Add the rice, parsley, coriander, cuminseed, turmeric, black pepper and remaining salt. With a wooden spoon, stir the eggs into the stuffing. Beat the mixture until well blended. Spoon the mixture into the zucchini, tomatoes and eggplants. Replace the tomato lids.

Place the stuffed vegetables in a shallow ovenproof dish. Spoon the melted butter over the vegetables. Place the dish in the oven and bake for 45 to 50 minutes, until vegetables and stuffing are tender. Remove the dish from the oven and serve the vegetables together on a large platter.

Part Four

COOKIES

For many children, the delectable aromas of home baking signal one thing—cookies. Nothing epitomizes homemade goodness better than freshly baked cookies, warm from the oven, rich with butter and set off with a tall glass of cold milk. They can be served with lemonade on a hot day or with hot chocolate on a frosty one. Cookies with ice cream make a special dessert or they can become an embellishment for a simple fruit dessert.

Cookies are one of the few foods best known in their homemade versions: crumbly oatmeal raisin, Toll House, large hermits and jumbles have all been favorites for years. Professionally produced cookies, called *petits fours secs* in French, are usually smaller and more delicate. These received their name, which means "small oven," because they were baked in the low heat of a cooled oven after the large cakes and tarts. Another type of *petits fours* are called *glacés,* or frosted, which are the small cakes called (somewhat confusingly) "petits fours" in English. Popular in French restaurants and *pâtisseries,* well-known examples of *petits fours secs* are *biscuits à la cuillère* (ladyfingers, often used in puddings and cakes), *palmiers* (palm leaves), and *madeleines,* the buttery cakes which sent Marcel Proust on a literary search for his lost remembrances.

Cookies, which are actually considered miniature cakes, have been made for centuries and often took on special cultural or religious significance. Some were used in ancient sacrifices and other religious ceremonies; several acquired special meaning as they became connected with the celebration of Christmas. Often, a cookie was a sign of good luck, a phenomenon we've all encountered when reading a "Chinese fortune cookie" at the end of a Chinese restaurant meal. The word "cookie" comes from the Dutch or Flemish *koekje,* meaning small cake; the word for cake being *koek.* What is a cookie to us is a biscuit to an Englishman. As to "cracker," the Oxford English Dictionary defines one as a "thin, hard biscuit" and notes that the term is used mostly in the United States.

The earliest cookies on record were used in sacrifices by the Egyptians. These small cakes were imprinted with horns to symbolize an ox, or cut in the shape of a man, and substituted for live sacrifices to the gods. Germanic tribes often did the same thing in times of poverty, when an ox could not be spared. These imprinted cookies were early versions of the popular *springerle* cakes.

Assyrians, Babylonians and Greeks all used cakes in religious ceremonies, the latter calling their mixture of fine flour and honey a *bouen,* which became the word bun. Shakespeare mentions cakes and ale, which were probably simple flour and water wafers.

Gingerbread is considered one of the earliest types of cookie known. Originally it was simply made with bread crumbs and honey. A more spicy version appeared in the Middle Ages, when ginger and pepper were frequently combined. The use of molasses as a familiar gingerbread ingredient was to come later, when the marvelously useful mellow syrup became available as a by-product of refined sugar.

Ginger cookies are popular in many cultures, including the Chinese (where one form of ginger wafer is called a "dot heart"), and our own, where gingersnaps and gingerbread men (and women) have earned a permanent niche in our baking repertoire.

Shortbread is another very old form of cookie. Traditional in Scotland, this rich, buttery cookie was probably a descendant of the Celtic oat bannock.

Lebkuchen, or German honey cakes, are another traditional form of cookie dating back many generations. These were made in cloisters during the Middle Ages; *leb* is derived from the Latin *libum,* a consecrated cake used in Roman religious ceremonies.

All around the world, wherever Christmas is celebrated, cookies play an important part. In Germany, some cookies are baked especially to be hung on the Christmas tree, and are shaped with a hole in their tops before baking to allow room for a colorful ribbon or silver or gold cord. Popular shapes include wreaths *(Berlinerkranzen* or *Vanillekranzen),* angels, small trees, stars *(Zimsterne),* candy canes twisted from two colors of dough, cookies cut to represent children, marzipan fruits, and pretzels *(Zitronenbrezeln* and *Vanillebrezeln).*

Sometimes cookies are painted with vegetable dyes, and a stained glass effect can be achieved by baking cookies with holes filled with crushed hard candies in bright colors.

Cookies are often classified into groups, according to the way they are shaped. One group is the family of bars and squares, formerly called "spread" cookies. This type of cookie is actually a small cake, the batter baked in a pan and then cut into bars or squares. The most familiar example is the brownie, an all-American favorite.

Brownies were first popular in the 1920s; they may have begun as a delicious fallen chocolate cake. First baked in Maine, brownies now appear in two forms, "fudgy" and "cakey," each with its adherents. Other popular members of this cookie group are lemon squares, date-nut bars, *Lebkuchen,* and Polish mazurka bars.

Probably the most familiar type of cookie is the drop cookie, which is formed by dropping small lumps of dough onto a baking sheet with 2 teaspoons. The all-time favorite drop cookie is undoubtedly the chocolate chip cookie, currently undergoing a huge resurgence in popularity. The original, of course, was the Toll House cookie, baked by Ruth Wakefield at the Toll House Inn in Whitman, Massachusetts, during the Depression. Most of us grew up with this same recipe, rich with brown sugar, nuts, and plenty of semisweet chocolate chips.

Hermits are another long-time favorite. Their origin is probably Cape Cod: because the spicy hermits kept well, they were packed along on long clipper journeys. They appear in a cookbook as early as the 1880s, and are still baked today.

Jumbles have been around since Colonial days, and appear in several nineteenth-century cookery books. Frequently, these formulas included applesauce, coconut, wine, buttermilk, dates and raisins. When ingredients were scarce during World War II, jumbles were baked with less butter, and with molasses instead of sugar.

There are possibly more varieties of drop cookies than any other group. These include florentines, peanut butter and molasses cookies, wafers with nuts, poppy seeds, or benne seeds (sesame seeds, popular in the Carolinas); macaroons made with bitter almonds (the Italian *amaretti,* or "little bitter things"), coconut, chocolate or pine nuts; *Pfeffernüsse,* snickerdoodles, *mostaccioli* (Neapolitan nut "moustaches"), *Anislaibchen* (German anise drops), and many more.

Rolled and molded cookies include several types. Some are rolled out like pastry, then cut into shapes. These include *Springerle,* shortbread, gingerbread men, sand tarts, stars, leaves and *speculaas* (popular in many countries, but particularly in Holland, where they take the form of windmills).

Molded cookies have the dough shaped before baking, usually by hand. Crescents *(Kipferl),* wreaths *(Kranzen),* and pretzels *(Brezeln)* are among the traditional shapes.

Sometimes the dough is shaped with a pastry bag, as for the famous French cookie, *langues de chats* (cats' tongues), or a press, as for *spritz* cookies in various shapes.

Refrigerator cookies such as pinwheels and nut crisps are made with a dough that is chilled in a long roll, and can then be sliced to produce the desired number of round wafers. There are also several kinds of filled cookies such as jam tarts and sandwiches.

An intriguing variation is the family of curled cookies. These are soft doughs that spread, when baked, into large, thin wafers. While still warm from the oven, they are quickly rolled or curled, sometimes around a form such as a metal cone or tube, or around the handle of a wooden spoon or broom. They are then crisp enough to be piped with a creamy filling. Scandinavian *krumkakor* fall into this group, as do *Frankfurter Oblaten* (sugar wafers), French *tuiles* ("roof tiles"), cigarettes, brandy snaps and nut wafers.

Cookies are not all alike. Some are made of few ingredients, simply shaped, and served without icing or decoration. Others are richly flavored, elaborately decorated, put together with filling to make sandwiches, made of many layers, or piped to make fancy shapes. Also, the dough is made in different ways and the cookies are formed by different methods.

Cookies can be elaborate or simple, but no matter what type of cookies you make, plan to use the best butter you can find, preferably unsalted. This is one time where nothing but the best will do.

Cookies are one of the most satisfactory baking projects a home baker can undertake. Even if the results are a little lopsided and the shapes not uniform, the cookies will taste delicious and will be eaten with delight.

COOKIES

Cookie flour is all-purpose flour. Unbleached flour has too much gluten and will tend to produce a tough cookie. Occasionally cornstarch or sweet rice flour is added to give the cookies a crumbly texture. Flour should always be sifted before you measure it, then sifted again with the other dry ingredients. In this way the measure will be exact, the texture lighter, and the ingredients will be easier to combine. A rising ingredient such as baking powder or soda is often used and should be sifted with the flour.

Salt, a natural complement to sugar, is used to bring out flavor and aid the baking process. A pinch (1/8 teaspoon) is sufficient for 2 cups of flour. Sift it with the flour.

Granulated or superfine sugar are the usual sweeteners; brown sugar is also often used. Your sugar should be sifted to be sure it is lump free. Honey and molasses are also used as sweeteners.

Unsalted butter is the best shortening for flavor and texture. Margarine can be substituted but there will be a slight loss in flavor. Vegetable shortening is sometimes used, but never

Basic Ingredients

The basic cookie ingredients are flour, sugar, shortening (usually unsalted butter), eggs, some liquid and a pinch of salt.

Rubbed-in Method Cookies

Makes 30 cookies

2	cups all-purpose flour
1/8	teaspoon salt
4	ounces unsalted butter
1/2	cup superfine sugar
1	large egg
1	teaspoon vanilla extract

1 Preheat oven to 325°F. Grease a large baking sheet and set aside.

2 Sift flour, salt, plus any dry spices or flavorings if used, into a large bowl. Cut butter into tiny pieces and add to flour.

6 Use a lightly floured rolling pin to roll out the dough to a sheet 1/8-inch thick.

7 Dip a 3-inch cookie cutter into flour; stamp out cookie rounds. Transfer rounds to greased baking sheet, allowing space.

8 For Linzer cookies, cut two rounds per cookie. Using a smaller cutter cut a hole in the center of one of the rounds.

alone. It should be combined with butter or margarine.

All eggs should be at room temperature for best results. They should be lightly beaten before being added to the dry ingredients. When an egg is not used, the cookie dough is bound with a liquid. This can be milk, fruit juice, coffee, water and sometimes wine.

Flavorings

Dried fruits, such as raisins, apricots, prunes and currants, can be mixed with the dry ingredients. Large pieces should be cut up with scissors or a knife. If the fruit is moist, such as dates, flour your knife.

Ground or finely chopped almonds, walnuts, hazelnuts are often used.

Grated lemon or orange rind is a lovely addition, imparting a tangy flavor. Use about 2 teaspoons for every 2 cups of flour.

Powdered cocoa is often used to give a chocolate flavor. Be sure to reduce the amount of sugar if it is sweetened cocoa.

Cinnamon, nutmeg, ginger, cloves and other spices are used for additional flavor. Be careful not to exceed 1 teaspoon for 2 cups of flour, and be sure the spices are fresh. Store them away from heat.

Equipment

Cookies do not require a lot of equipment; measuring cups and spoons, rolling pin, a mixing bowl, a wire cooling rack and baking sheets are enough for most cookies. The baking sheets should be fairly heavy, preferably

3 Rub butter into the flour until the mixture resembles bread crumbs. Stir in the sugar and make a well in the center.

4 Beat egg lightly with vanilla. Pour it into the well and draw dry ingredients into the egg with a fork, until mixture sticks together.

5 Knead gently until mixture forms a smooth ball, then turn out on a lightly floured board.

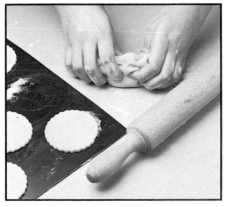

9 Pat dough scraps into a ball, roll out again, and cut out remaining cookies. Transfer to the baking sheet.

10 Prick surface of cookies with a fork, or brush with egg white or egg yolk and sprinkle with sugar.

11 Bake on the center shelf of the oven for 13 to 15 minutes. After 5 minutes, transfer to a wire rack to cool.

aluminum, and of a size that allows 1-inch clearance on all sides when placed in the oven. In addition you will need a spatula to remove baked cookies from the baking sheet.

Cookie cutters are also useful tools. These should be of metal rather than plastic. If they are tinned metal, be sure they are dried thoroughly after use or they may rust.

For decorative cookies, you will need a pastry bag. The newer ones are made of nylon, which is easy to clean and drys quickly, or plastic. You should also have a variety of tips to permit different shapes and designs.

Other equipment might be a shortbread mold, madeleine tins, fancy rolling pins for making springerle cookies, gingerbread, animal figures, etc.

Basic Method

Sift the flour before it is measured and resift it with the salt and spices, etc. Sugar should be free of lumps, particu-larly important in the case of brown sugar or confectioners' (powdered) sugar.

The butter should be firm if you are making cookies by the "rubbed-in" method (similar to pastry) or softened if you are making cookies by the creamed method.

The eggs should be at room temperature and should be beaten lightly before being added to the mixture.

The oven should be preheated; the temperature varies with the recipe.

Creamed Method

1 Arrange shelves in oven; for one sheet, center shelf; for two, arrange one above and one below center. Grease baking sheet.

2 Sift flour and other dry ingredients and set aside. Beat softened butter with a wooden spoon until light and creamy.

3 Add sugar to butter and continue creaming until mixture is light in color, fluffy in texture, and the sugar no longer grainy.

6 Stir in the sifted flour, beating vigorously, until it is thoroughly incorporated with the creamed mixture.

7 Drop batter by spoonful onto greased baking sheet, pushing it off with another spoon. Drop the mounds 2 inches apart.

OR Spoon batter into a piping bag fitted with a star tip and pipe out star-shaped mounds on the baking sheet.

Place a single baking sheet on the center shelf. If you have 2 sheets, place one on each shelf, positioning them just above and below the center, and change the sheets halfway through the baking time. If you have more than 2 sheets, bake the batches in sequence; don't try to bake more than 2 sheets at once. Allow 15 minutes to preheat the oven. Most cookies are baked at moderate temperatures. Buttery doughs are usually baked at lower temperatures.

Types of Cookies

Drop Cookies. The dough is scooped up with a spoon and dropped onto the baking sheet or pushed off the spoon with a second spoon or a small rubber spatula.

Hand-Molded Cookies. The dough is measured and shaped by hand into round or oval balls, usually about 1 inch in diameter. These are then flattened, often with the tines of a fork.

Pan-Molded Cookies. The dough is pressed into small molds of special shapes. Madeleines, the famous cookies that started Proust's chain of memories, are a good example.

Cutout Cookies. These are made of a fairly stiff dough, which is rolled out to a thin sheet; the exact thickness depends on the recipe. The cookies are stamped out with cutters of various sizes and shapes, or with a pastry wheel. For rectangular or square

---

OR With an electric mixer, place butter and sugar together in the bowl and cream together with the machine.

4 If recipe uses whole egg, beat lightly, then add to creamed mixture. If using yolks alone, drop directly into bowl and mix.

5 Use a rubber spatula to scrape the mixture down the sides of the bowl and spoon, and beat again.

OR Roll out the dough to a ¼-inch-thick sheet and cut out cookies. Place them on the baking sheet 1 inch apart.

OR Press the dough into a greased square or rectangular baking pan; smooth top with a spatula.

8 Bake cookies for 10 to 20 minutes, according to recipe. Cut into bars if you baked dough in pan. Cool cookies on wire rack.

shapes, a sharp knife can be used. Cut-outs can be used for filled sandwiches, too, or bulls' eyes, which have a hole in the center of the top piece to reveal the filling.

Refrigerator Cookies. These are made of a dough too soft to roll. The whole batch of dough is shaped into a log, round or oval in cross-section, or into a square, and chilled until firm. The chilled dough is cut into thin slices with a sharp knife.

Piped Cookies. The batter for these is spooned into a pastry bag. It is piped out in various shapes, depending on the tip you use on the piping bag. Ladyfingers and star-shaped meringues are familiar examples.

Pressed Cookies. These are made of a rather stiff dough, which is spooned into a press. The shape and size are determined by the press; variations are limited.

Bar Cookies. These are baked in flat cake pans, usually square or rectangular, and are cut into pieces after baking. Often the dough is made of several layers.

Wafers and Cookies Shaped after Baking. These delicate cookies need special care. They are very thin and usually large. When they are baked, they are still soft and flexible; in this stage they are rolled or curled or shaped around molds. As soon as the cookie is shaped and cooled, it becomes firm and crisp. When they are rolled into cones or tubes, they are sometimes filled.

Petits fours secs. These are fancy cookies, baked very small and generally more elaborately flavored and decorated than ordinary cookies. The types are varied: crisp buttery crescents, elegant curved *tuiles d'amandes,* chocolate-tipped *langues de chats.* As well as being served with coffee, these are perfect for an afternoon tea party. They are also a fine complement for sherry or Madeira.

Mixing Cookie Doughs

Cookie doughs are mixed in several different ways.

Rubbed-in Method. The shortening is rubbed into the flour in the same way that is used in making pastry. This method is used for some cut-out cookies. The shortening should be quite firm when it is cut into the flour and it should be mixed or rubbed until it resembles fine bread crumbs. For a richer dough, such as shortbread, the proportion of butter is higher and consequently the crumbs will be larger. If you are adding fruit, nuts or citrus rind, stir into the mixture at this point with the sugar.

If an egg is being used to bind the mixture, beat it lightly with a fork before adding it to the other ingredients. To add the liquid or egg, make a well in the center of the mixture and pour in. Use a fork to draw the dry ingredients into the liquid with a stirring motion, until the mixture sticks together in the bowl to form a stiff dough.

When the mixture sticks together in a ball, knead it gently until the ball is smooth and free from cracks. This light kneading is essential to make the mixture roll out evenly and smoothly. If the dough is too soft to roll, wrap it in foil or wax paper and refrigerate until firm.

The next stage is the rolling of the dough. This is best done on either a wooden board or smooth work surface. Dust the surface lightly with flour to prevent sticking. The rolling pin should be lightly floured as well. Rolling in one direction, roll out the dough to the thickness called for in the recipe.

To prevent sticking, lightly flour the cutter of your choice. Cut out the cookies in one firm press to get a clean cut. Using a spatula, transfer the cutout cookies to a greased baking sheet. Gather the dough scraps into a ball and roll the ball out to cut more cookies. Continue until you have used all the dough.

The cookies may be brushed with lightly beaten egg and sprinkled with chopped nuts, poppy or caraway seeds before baking.

When all the cookies are cut out, you can prick the surface of plain, flat ones with a fork. This gives a decorative finish and also helps them to bake evenly. Place the baking sheet in the center of the oven. If using 2 sheets, place one above center and the other below center.

Depending on the amount of butter used, the cookies may still be soft when they come out of the oven. They firm very quickly. Allow them to set on the baking sheet for 5 minutes before transferring. Cool on a wire rack. Make sure the cookies are absolutely cold before storing in airtight containers.

Creamed Method. In this method, the butter, softened to room temperature, is beaten until smooth and creamy. The sugar is added and the creaming process continued until the sugar is completely dissolved. Then beat in liquid flavorings or citrus rind, if called for by the recipe. Eggs which have been beaten lightly are then added gradually. Flour and other dry ingredients can now be added to the creamed mixture all at once and stirred in until thoroughly incorporated.

Melted Method. In this method the shortening and very often the sweetening ingredient are melted together without allowing the mixture to come to a boil. Be sure the mixture has cooled before adding any eggs. The next step is to add all the dry ingredients to the pan at once and gently stir into the melted mixture until smoothly blended.

Cookies made by the melted method will still be soft when they are baked; leave them on the baking sheet for 2 minutes, then transfer to racks; they will become firm as they cool. Bar cookies are allowed to cool for up to 30 minutes before they are removed from the pan.

Wafers that are rolled or shaped after baking require careful attention. As soon as the cookies are baked, while still warm, lift them off the sheet, and roll and shape as quickly as possible. If the cookies begin to cool and harden, slide the baking sheet into the oven again to warm and soften them.

Shaping Cookies Made by Melted Method

• The melted method is used to combine shortening with a heavy sweetener such as honey or molasses, or to melt chocolate.

• Be sure the mixture is cooled somewhat before combining it with egg. Otherwise the egg will cook and not blend in.

1 For bar cookies, spread dough in a square or rectangular baking pan. After baking, while mixture is still warm, cut into bars.

1 For round cookies, mold by hand into walnut-size balls. Place balls 1 to 1½ inches apart on the baking sheet.

1 For drop cookies, drop mixture, 1 teaspoon at a time, onto baking sheet, allowing 3 to 4 inches between the mounds of dough.

1 For rolled wafers, oil the handle of a wooden spoon. Use a spatula to lift still hot and flexible wafers, top side down, onto a board.

2 Place handle on edge near you and roll up the wafer. Slip out the handle. If wafers become too hard to roll, return to oven briefly.

OR Wrap the wafers around cornet molds to make cream horns. Fill with fruit and cream or with ice cream.

OR Make baskets to hold cold desserts (ice cream, mousse, etc.) by shaping the wafer around a well-oiled ramekin, or orange.

OR Shape a large basket. Bake an extra-large wafer and shape around an oiled cake pan or bowl. Fill with fruit or cold dessert.

40 tiny cookies

Basic Mixture

1	tablespoon soft butter
1⅓	cups (4 ounces) ground blanched almonds (see Note)
½	cup superfine sugar
2	medium-size egg yolks
1	drop of almond extract

• Chocolatines. Cut 1-inch squares, sandwich with a chocolate filling. Coat with chocolate icing and sprinkle with chopped blanched almonds.
• Mochatines. Cut 1-inch rounds, sandwich with coffee buttercream. Spread top and sides with more buttercream, and roll sides in chopped nuts.
• Apricotines. Cut shapes to your taste, sandwich with strained apricot jam. Coat with fondant and roll in chopped nuts.
• Minstrels. Cut 1-inch squares. Dip them into melted dark chocolate and let it set. Pipe wavy lines of milk chocolate on top.
Note: Ground almonds are available in a 6-ounce package (2 cups). Otherwise, grind blanched whole almonds in a food processor or blender.

1 Preheat oven to 400°F. Adjust racks, one above center, one below center. Brush 2 baking sheets with melted butter.

2 Put ground almonds in a bowl and stir in the sugar. Make a well in the center.

1 *Cherry Flutes:* Roll out the mixture to a sheet ¼-inch thick.

2 Use a floured 1¾-inch scalloped cutter to cut out 10 circles from each portion of dough. Brush with beaten egg.

1 *Almond Flakies:* Use a heart-shaped cutter (or other fancy shape) to cut out 10 cookies from each portion of dough.

2 Brush each cookie with beaten egg and sprinkle with chopped or flaked blanched almonds.

1 *Chocolate Sticks:* Roll out each portion of dough to a 4-inch square.

3 Add egg yolks and almond extract. Mix ingredients to form a stiff paste.

4 Lightly flour a wooden board. Turn the dough onto the board and knead until smooth and pliable.

5 Divide the dough into 4 parts to make different cookies, or use the whole batch to make any kind you prefer.

3 Place a halved glacéed cherry, cut side down, on each circle. Pinch the dough around the cherry.

1 *Silver Rings:* Using the same scalloped cutter, cut out 10 circles from each portion of dough.

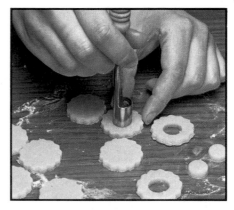

2 Use a small cutter or a thimble to cut out the center of each round.

2 Use a sharp knife to cut dough into 8 to 10 thin strips, taking care not to pull the pastry.

3 Bake all the shapes for 5 minutes, until lightly browned. Cool. Finish silver rings with confectioners' sugar icing.

4 Dip chocolate sticks, both ends, into melted chocolate, then into chopped nuts.

Scottish Shortbread

6 to 8 pieces

- ¾ cup all-purpose flour
- ⅓ cup rice flour
  pinch of salt
- ¼ cup granulated sugar
- 4 ounces unsalted butter

• Rice flour is used in shortbread, because it gives lighter, crisper results. If you cannot obtain this, use all-purpose flour instead.

• The sugar is added before the butter as the mixture is too dense to add sugar after the butter has been rubbed in.

1 Preheat oven to 325°F. If using a mold or a 7-inch cake pan, dust lightly with rice flour. The baking sheet should not be greased.

2 Sift the 2 flours and the salt into a large bowl. Stir in the sugar and mix thoroughly.

3 Cut the butter into the flour until the mixture has the consistency of large bread crumbs.

4 Knead the mixture into a smooth crack-free ball. If the dough becomes sticky, cover the bowl and refrigerate it for 10 minutes.

5 Press the shortbread into the mold or cake pan with the palm of your hand.

6 If using a mold, hold it close to the baking sheet, tap the base and the shortbread will come out.

7 If using a cake pan, turn out the round onto the baking sheet and flute the edge, using your fingers or the handle of a teaspoon.

8 Use a sharp knife to mark the round on top into portions. Do not cut through.

9 Bake on the middle level of the oven for about 45 minutes, until the shortbread is pale gold in color.

10 Cool on the baking sheet for 10 minutes before transferring to a wire rack. Sprinkle sugar on top and cut into wedges.

Tuiles d'Amande
(Almond Wafers)

45 cookies

4	tablespoons unsalted butter, softened	⅓	cup finely ground almonds
½	cup granulated sugar	½	teaspoon vanilla extract
2	egg whites	¼	teaspoon almond extract (optional)
5	tablespoons *unsifted* cake flour (not self-rising)	½	cup sliced or slivered almonds

Preheat oven to 325°F. Place the rack on the middle level. Lightly butter 2 baking sheets. You can prepare and fill the 2 sheets but you should only bake one at a time.

Cream the softened butter with the sugar and beat until the mixture is soft and fluffy. Add the egg whites, beating for just a few seconds to blend them in. Sift the flour over the batter and fold it in with a rubber spatula. Fold in the ground almonds and the extracts.

Using a spoon and a rubber spatula, scoop up ½ teaspoons of the batter; a demitasse spoon is the perfect size. Scrape the batter 3 inches apart onto a baking sheet. With the dampened back of a spoon, spread the batter out to a diameter of about 2½ inches; it will be very thin. Top each one with a sprinkling of the sliced or slivered almonds.

Bake until the edges are slightly browned; it may only take about 4 or 5 minutes, depending on the thickness of the cookie.

The rounded shape of the cookies is formed by placing them on a rolling pin, straight-sided bottle, inverted large ring mold, long thick wooden dowel, or anything else you can think of. They become crisp very quickly so you have to work fast while they are hot, placing them face up on your rolling pin, or other mold, one at a time. As the first cakes harden into shape, remove them to make room for the later ones.

When the cookies are done, remove cookie sheet from the oven. Rest the sheet on the open oven door, if possible; this will keep the cookies warm. Quickly lift one off the sheet with a flexible spatula and place it face up on the rounded surface. Continue working fast, removing and forming the remaining cookies. If they have cooled too much to shape, return them to the oven for a few seconds to soften them.

Close the oven door and allow a few minutes for the temperature to return to 325°F. Continue baking and shaping the remainder of the cookies. Store them airtight.

Variations:
1. Eliminate the finely ground almonds, add the grated rind of ½ orange, and blend in the slivered almonds instead of sprinkling them on top.
2. Substitute 1 cup chopped walnuts, reduce the flour to ¼ cup, and add 2 tablespoons cream and 1 tablespoon liqueur or rum.
3. Reduce the flour to 3 tablespoons. Use 1 cup finely chopped (rice-size pieces) almonds and 1 whole egg; increase the vanilla to 1 teaspoon. Bake at 375°F for 8 to 10 minutes. Cookies are formed from 1½ teaspoons of batter; flatten them with the tines of a fork.

Langues de Chats
(Cats' Tongues)

36 cookies

4	ounces unsalted butter	2	egg whites
½	cup granulated sugar	⅓	cup unsifted all-purpose flour
⅛	teaspoon vanilla extract		

Preheat oven to 400°F. Adjust the racks, placing one above the center and the other below the center. Butter and flour 2 baking sheets; shake off the excess flour.

Cream the butter until it is very soft and fluffy. Add the sugar gradually and beat in the vanilla. The mixture should be very light and soft. Beat the egg whites very briefly with a fork. Add about 1 tablespoon of the whites at a time, folding them in quickly and lightly with a rubber spatula. Don't try to mix them in completely. Sift about one quarter of the flour over the batter and quickly cut it in with the spatula; repeat until all the flour has been just cut in.

Fit a pastry bag with a plain tube, about ⅜ inch in diameter, # 4, and fill it about two thirds full. Pipe the batter onto the sheets in strips 3-inches long and the thickness of a finger. Leave about 3 inches of space between them as they spread a lot.

Bake them for 8 to 10 minutes, until the thin edge of the cookies has browned. Check the oven after about 6 minutes, but do not reverse the sheets unless they are browning very unevenly. Cool on wire racks.

If you wish to make the cats' tongues a bit more elegant, dip the ends into melted chocolate. Melt 3 ounces (3 squares) bittersweet or semisweet chocolate in a bowl over hot water. When the cookies are completely cool, dip each end into the melted chocolate.

Cigarettes Russes

18 cookies

1	tablespoon softened butter	2	large egg whites	
4	tablespoons unsalted butter	1/8	teaspoon cream of tartar	
1/3	cup plus 1 teaspoon all-purpose flour	1/2	cup granulated sugar	
		2	or 3 drops of vanilla extract	

Preheat oven to 350°F. Place the rack on the middle level. Use the tablespoon of softened butter to grease 2 baking sheets; you will, however, only bake one sheet at a time.

Melt the 4 tablespoons butter and set aside. Sift the flour onto a piece of wax paper and set aside. Place the egg whites in a large bowl, preferably unlined copper. If you do not have a copper bowl you will need to add the cream of tartar to the egg whites when beating them. This helps them mount and stabilizes them. With a large balloon whisk or a hand-held beater, start beating the egg whites, adding the cream of tartar if necessary. Beat until the egg whites are creamy and smooth, then gradually add the sugar and vanilla while continuing to beat. When the egg whites are forming soft peaks, gradually add the melted butter and sifted flour.

Spread tablespoons of the mixture in small oblongs on one of the prepared sheets, smoothing them into a rectangular shape. Leave about 3 inches between them.

Bake on the middle level for 7 to 8 minutes, until golden brown. You can prepare the second sheet while the first batch is baking. When the cookies are done, remove the tray from the oven. Do not turn the oven off.

Working quickly, remove 1 cookie from the sheet with a large spatula and place it upside down on a flat surface. Quickly wind the cookie around a pencil or chopstick. Slide it onto a wire rack to cool. Continue shaping the cigarettes. If they become too hard to roll, return them to the oven briefly to soften them.

Black Pepper Cookies

36 cookies

6	ounces plus 1 teaspoon unsalted butter	1	cup sugar	
3/4	teaspoon freshly ground black pepper	1	large egg	
3/4	teaspoon ground cinnamon	1 1/2	cups all-purpose flour	
1/4	teaspoon ground cloves	2	teaspoons baking powder	
1 1/2	teaspoons vanilla extract	1/4	teaspoon salt	
		3/4	cup cocoa powder	

Preheat oven to 375°F. Coat 2 baking sheets with the teaspoon of butter.

Blend remaining 6 ounces butter, the spices and vanilla together in a large bowl. Gradually add sugar, then the egg; beat until light and creamy. Sift together flour, baking powder, salt and cocoa. Stir into the creamed mixture until a stiff dough is formed.

With floured hands, form the dough into 1-inch balls. Place the balls 1 1/2 inches apart on the buttered baking sheets. Gently flatten each ball to 1/4-inch thickness.

Bake cookies for 12 minutes. Transfer to a wire rack to cool completely.

Wine Cookies

30 to 35 cookies

2/3	cup dried currants	1 1/2	teaspoons ground cinnamon	
1/2	cup sweet white wine	3/4	cup sugar	
6	ounces plus 2 teaspoons unsalted butter	2	eggs	
3	cups all-purpose flour			

Soak currants in the wine for 1 hour. Coat 2 baking sheets with the 2 teaspoons butter. Sift flour and cinnamon together and set aside. Preheat oven to 375°F.

Cream 6 ounces butter and the sugar together in a large mixing bowl until light and fluffy. Beat in the eggs, one at a time. Blend in the flour mixture, then the currants and wine.

Drop the batter by heaping teaspoons on the buttered cookie sheets; space mounds well apart and smooth the tops. Bake cookies until golden, 15 to 20 minutes. Cool on the baking sheets for 5 minutes, then transfer to racks to cool completely.

Linzer Cookies

20 cookies

1 cup all-purpose flour	6 tablespoons unsalted butter
½ teaspoon baking powder	⅓ cup granulated sugar
⅛ teaspoon salt	1 egg, lightly beaten
¼ teaspoon ground cinnamon	8 tablespoons raspberry jam
¼ teaspoon ground cloves	confectioners' sugar

Preheat oven to 325°F. Butter 2 large baking sheets. Sift flour, baking powder, salt and spices into a bowl. Cut in the butter until the pieces are the size of small peas. Rub the mixture between the fingers until it resembles bread crumbs. Stir in the granulated sugar. Make a well in the center of the mixture and pour in the egg. Work with a fork, mixing the dry ingredients into the egg, until a smooth dough is formed.

Roll out the dough on a floured board to ⅛-inch thickness. Using a 2½-inch cookie cutter, cut out 40 circles. Reroll the scraps of dough as necessary to make all the circles. With a smaller cutter, cut out the centers of half of the circles.

Bake the cookies until lightly browned, 10 to 12 minutes. Cool them on the cookie sheets for 5 minutes, then transfer to wire racks to cool completely.

Spread each whole cookie with about 1 teaspoon of the jam. Sprinkle the cutout cookie tops with confectioners' sugar. Place a cutout on top of each jam-covered round. Fill in the hole with more jam.

Florentines

18 to 20 cookies

7 tablespoons unsalted butter	½ cup glacé cherries, chopped
¼ cup honey	¾ cup slivered blanched almonds
¼ cup firmly packed brown sugar	1 teaspoon fresh lemon juice
2 tablespoons all-purpose flour	4 ounces semisweet chocolate (4 squares)
¼ cup seedless golden raisins	

Preheat oven to 350°F. Melt 1 tablespoon of the butter and brush it over 2 baking sheets.

Cut remaining 6 tablespoons butter into pieces; place in a saucepan with the honey and brown sugar. Stir over low heat until the butter melts. Cool mixture slightly, then sift the flour into the mixture and stir in. Mix in raisins, cherries, almonds and lemon juice.

Drop batter by heaping teaspoons 4 inches apart onto the buttered baking sheets. Bake for 15 minutes. Cool on the baking sheets for 5 minutes, then transfer to wire racks to cool completely.

Melt the chocolate in the top pan of a double boiler over very hot water. Remove the pan from heat and let the chocolate cool until thickened. Spread the bottom of each cookie with chocolate. Place cookies, chocolate side up, on wire racks. When chocolate is nearly set, decorate with wavy lines made with the tines of a fork. Let chocolate set completely.

Zürich Hazelnut Rounds

20 cookies

4 tablespoons plus 2
  teaspoons unsalted
  butter
1 cup all-purpose flour
1 egg, lightly beaten
1 cup ground blanched
  hazelnuts

Icing

½ cup sugar
3 ounces semisweet
  chocolate (3 squares)
¼ cup water
3 tablespoons apricot jam
20 whole blanched hazelnuts

Preheat oven to 300°F. Use 1 teaspoon of the butter to coat 2 baking sheets. Beat 4 tablespoons butter and the flour in a large mixing bowl until well combined. Stir in the beaten egg, ground hazelnuts and 6 tablespoons of the sugar; mix well.

On a lightly floured surface, roll out the dough to ⅛-inch thickness. With a 2-inch cookie cutter, cut dough into circles. Place the circles on the buttered baking sheets. Bake them until lightly browned, 20 to 25 minutes. Cool on wire racks.

Prepare the icing: Melt the chocolate in the top pan of a double boiler over very hot water. Combine remaining 2 tablespoons sugar and ¼ cup water in a small saucepan. Boil, stirring constantly, until a thick syrup is formed. Pour the syrup into the melted chocolate; add remaining 1 teaspoon butter. Stir until icing is well blended.

Sandwich the cookies together with apricot jam, using about ½ teaspoon for each one. Spread icing over the tops. Garnish each round with a whole hazelnut.

Hazelnut Bars

8 to 10 bars

4 tablespoons unsalted
  butter
½ cup granulated sugar
1 small egg

¾ cup self-rising cake flour
  (see Note)
2 ounces hazelnuts, ground

Preheat oven to 350°F. Grease a 7-inch-square pan. Cream the butter until soft. Add the sugar and continue to cream until the mixture is light and smooth. Lightly beat the egg and add it to the mixture. Sift the flour into the mixture and stir it in. Add the hazelnuts, mixing them in lightly.

Spread the mixture in an even layer in the prepared pan. Bake for about 25 minutes. Allow the cake to cool for about 5 minutes. Cut into bars and transfer them to a rack to cool.

Note: If you do not have self-rising cake flour, substitute plain cake flour or all-purpose flour and add 1 teaspoon baking powder.

Chocolate Chip Nut Bars

40 bars

2½ cups sifted all-purpose
  flour
½ teaspoon salt
4 ounces unsalted butter
1½ cups firmly packed dark
  brown sugar

3 large eggs
1 teaspoon vanilla extract
6 ounces semisweet
  chocolate bits
4 ounces shelled pecans or
  walnuts, chopped (1 cup)

Preheat oven to 350°F. Place the rack on the middle level. Butter a jelly-roll pan, 10 × 15 inches. Sift the flour with the salt. Cream the butter until it is soft. Add the brown sugar and continue to cream until light and smooth. Add the eggs, one at a time, beating after each addition, and stir in the vanilla.

Gradually add the flour, blending it well; finally fold in the chocolate and the nuts.

Spread the batter evenly in the prepared pan. Bake for 30 to 35 minutes. The top should spring back gently when touched. Cool the cake in the pan on a rack before cutting it into bars, 1½ × 2 inches.

Brandy Snaps

*These curled cookies are often served filled with
sweetened whipped cream.*

36 cookies

1 cup sifted all-purpose flour	⅔ cup granulated sugar
1½ teaspoons ground ginger	4 ounces unsalted butter, cut
½ cup light molasses, or ¼	into small bits
cup dark molasses and	1 tablespoon brandy
¼ cup light corn syrup	

Preheat oven to 300°F. Adjust the racks to divide the oven into thirds. Butter 2 baking sheets, 12 × 16 inches. Sift the flour before measuring and resift with the ginger. In a heavy saucepan heat the molasses, or molasses and corn syrup, with the sugar and cut-up butter until syrup is hot and butter melted. Remove from heat. Add the flour and ginger gradually, beating until smooth. As the mixture cools, it will thicken slightly. Beat in the brandy.

Drop by teaspoons very far apart, placing about six on a baking sheet. Snaps will spread during baking. Bake them for 10 to 12 minutes, until they are light brown. About halfway through the baking time, reverse the baking sheets from the upper to the lower rack and turn them from front to back. If you are not practiced at rolling cookies, you may prefer to bake 1 sheet at a time; use the center level of the oven in that case.

Remove baking sheets from the oven and let them cool for a minute before attempting to remove the cookies. Remove them one at a time, but work quickly while they are still warm. Place a cookie face down on your work surface, place the round handle of a wooden spoon at the edge of the cookie nearest you and loosely roll the cookie around the handle. Immediately slide the cookie off the handle and place it on a board to cool. Continue to form the cookies in this fashion. If they cool too much and become too crisp, return them to the oven briefly.

If the cookies are to be filled, you will need a larger round than a spoon handle. Some hardware stores (and any lumberyard) sell wooden dowels 1 inch in diameter. The cookies soften easily and must be stored airtight to remain crisp. If they are to be filled, it should be done just before serving them.

Coffee Whirls

24 sandwich cookies

2 cups all-purpose flour
¼ teaspoon salt
8 ounces unsalted butter

1 tablespoon instant coffee powder
1 teaspoon boiling water
¼ cup powdered sugar

Filling

6 tablespoons unsalted butter
1 teaspoon instant coffee powder

1 tablespoon hot milk
1¼ cups powdered sugar

Preheat oven to 375°F. Adjust the racks, placing them one above the center and the other below the center. Lightly grease 2 baking sheets. Sift the flour before measuring and stir in the salt. Cream the butter until soft. Dissolve the instant coffee in the boiling water and beat into the butter. Add the powdered sugar and cream until smooth. Add the flour and salt, and blend well.

Using a pastry bag fitted with a ½-inch star nozzle, pipe the mixture into rounds on the prepared baking sheets. You should have 48 rounds.

Bake for about 12 minutes. Halfway through the baking time, reverse the baking sheets from top to bottom and from front to back.

While the cookies are baking, prepare the filling. Cream the butter until soft. Dissolve the instant coffee in the hot milk and add it. Beat in the powdered sugar until the mixture is smooth.

When the cookies are done, leave them on the sheets for about 5 minutes. Transfer them to a rack to cool. When they are completely cold, put the coffee filling between pairs of cookies to form a sandwich.

Peanut Butter Cookies

This large batch of dough can be divided. Freeze half for future baking.

72 cookies

2¾ cups sifted all-purpose flour
1½ teaspoons baking soda
¼ teaspoon salt
4 ounces unsalted butter
1 cup granulated sugar

1 cup firmly packed brown sugar, light or dark
2 eggs
1 cup peanut butter, preferably crunchy
½ teaspoon vanilla extract

Sift flour before measuring and resift it with the baking soda and salt. Cream the butter until soft; add both sugars and beat until light and fluffy. Add the eggs, one at a time, beating well after each addition. Beat in the peanut butter and the vanilla. Gradually add the sifted dry ingredients until just blended. Refrigerate the dough for about 2 hours.

Preheat oven to 375°F. Adjust the racks to divide the oven into thirds. Butter 2 baking sheets, or line them with foil. Using a lightly rounded teaspoon as a measure, shape the dough into 1-inch balls by rolling it between your hands. Place the balls 3 inches apart on the baking sheets, and flatten them lightly with a fork dipped into cold water. Make a crisscross design with the tines of the fork.

Bake the cookies for 10 to 12 minutes, or until golden in color. After about 6 minutes, reverse the cookie sheets from the upper to the lower rack and turn them from front to back at the same time. Cool on a rack.

96

Lace Cookies

24 cookies

4 ounces unsalted butter	1 tablespoon flour
½ cup granulated sugar	2 tablespoons cherry liqueur
½ cup ground blanched almonds	or orange liqueur

Preheat oven to 350°F. Butter and flour 2 baking sheets, shaking off excess flour. Or line them with foil and cut extra sheets of foil the size of the baking sheets. In a heavy saucepan or skillet combine the butter, sugar, almonds and flour over moderate heat, stirring, until the butter is completely melted. Remove from heat and stir in the liqueur.

Using a teaspoon and a rubber spatula, or the back of a second teaspoon, place the batter on the baking sheets, allowing 4 inches of space between them; they spread during baking. Form additional cookies on 2 sheets of foil. Bake for 6 to 7 minutes, until golden brown and bubbly. Let them stand no more than 1 minute before removing to a rack to cool.

You can curl these, if you like, over a rolling pin or the handle of a wooden spoon while they are still warm and soft, same technique as for Brandy Snaps (see index). If they cool too fast to curl, return them to the oven briefly to soften. Cool them seam side down on a rack. Slide the baking sheets under the filled foil sheets and continue baking and curling. Store airtight.

Burnt Butter Biscuits

30 cookies

1¼ cups all-purpose flour	1 large egg, lightly beaten
½ teaspoon baking powder	30 almond halves, about 2 ounces
4 ounces unsalted butter	
½ cup granulated sugar	

Preheat oven to 350°F. Adjust the racks, placing them one above the center level and the other below. Lightly butter 2 baking sheets. Sift the flour before measuring and resift it with the baking powder. Cut the butter into small pieces and place them in a heavy-bottomed pan over moderate heat. Watching carefully, allow the butter to melt and turn pale golden brown in color. Do not let it become dark brown or burned. Remove the butter from the heat and add the sugar, stirring gently. Allow to cool slightly. Add the beaten egg and gradually beat in the sifted flour.

Drop batter by teaspoons about 3 inches apart on the prepared baking sheets. Top each with an almond half.

Bake for 12 to 15 minutes, or until golden. Halfway through the baking time reverse the baking sheets from top to bottom and from front to back. Leave on the baking sheets for 2 or 3 minutes before transferring them to a rack to cool.

Lemon Bars

These have a lovely tang to them. Use fresh lemon juice only or the flavor is just not the same.

48 squares, 1½-inch size

4 ounces unsalted butter	¾ cup granulated sugar
¼ cup confectioners' sugar	2 eggs, beaten
1 cup sifted all-purpose flour	2 tablespoons all-purpose flour
2 tablespoons fresh lemon juice	½ teaspoon baking powder
grated rind of 1 lemon	⅓ cup sliced almonds

Preheat oven to 350°F, placing a rack on the middle level. Butter a pan 9 × 13 inches. Cream 4 ounces butter with ¼ cup confectioners' sugar and beat in the sifted 1 cup flour. Put into the greased pan, leveling it with a flexible spatula, or pat it level with wet hands. Bake for 15 minutes. Remove the pan from oven to cool slightly. Do not turn off the oven.

While the pastry is cooling, mix the lemon juice, grated rind and granulated sugar. Beat in the eggs. Combine 2 tablespoons flour and the baking powder and sift the mixture over the sugar and eggs, mixing it very well. Spread this over the cooled pastry. Top with the almonds and return the pan to the oven. Bake for 20 to 25 minutes longer.

Allow the pastry to cool before cutting into bars or squares.

Lady Biscuits

36 cookies

2¼ cups sifted all-purpose flour	⅔ cup granulated sugar
¼ teaspoon salt	3 egg whites
8 ounces unsalted butter	1 teaspoon vanilla extract

Preheat oven to 375°F. Adjust the racks to divide the oven into thirds. Use an additional teaspoon of butter to grease 2 baking sheets. Sift the flour before measuring and resift it with the salt. Cream the butter until soft and beat in the sugar until light and fluffy. Beat the egg whites lightly and add them along with the vanilla. Quickly fold in the flour and salt.

With lightly floured hands, form the dough into 36 small balls. If the dough seems too soft, refrigerate it until firm.

Place the balls about 3 inches apart on the prepared baking sheets. Flatten each ball with the back of a fork.

Bake for 12 to 15 minutes, or until the cookies are golden brown. After 8 or 9 minutes, reverse the sheets from the upper to the lower rack and turn them from front to back. Let them stand on the baking sheets for 2 or 3 minutes before transferring them to a rack to cool.

Toffee Bars

Thin and slightly chewy, this recipe yields a large batch.

40 large or 80 small bars

2 cups sifted all-purpose flour
8 ounces unsalted butter
1 cup firmly packed dark brown sugar

1 teaspoon vanilla extract
6 ounces semisweet chocolate bits (1 cup)
1 cup chopped walnuts

Preheat oven to 350°F. Place a rack on the middle level. Lightly butter a jelly-roll pan, 10 × 15 inches. Sift the flour before measuring. Cream the butter and brown sugar until light and fluffy; beat in the vanilla. Add the flour gradually, beating until just mixed. Stir in the chocolate bits and walnuts.

Spread the mixture, which will be stiff, in the prepared pan and level it with the back of a wet flexible spatula. You can also pat it level with your hands; keep running them over an ice cube and they will stay cool and wet, preventing sticking.

Bake for about 25 minutes, or until nicely browned and faintly crusted. Let the cake cool slightly before cutting it with a thin sharp knife into 2-inch squares or 1 × 2-inch bars. Let them cool before removing from the pan.

Variation: Omit the chocolate chips and add 1 cup raisins.

Jinny's Gingersnaps

36 cookies

2 cups sifted all-purpose flour
1 teaspoon baking soda
1½ teaspoons ground ginger
½ teaspoon grated nutmeg or mace

½ teaspoon ground cinnamon
¼ teaspoon ground cloves
5½ ounces unsalted butter
⅔ cup sugar
¼ cup dark molasses
1 teaspoon vanilla extract

Sift the flour before measuring and resift it with the baking soda and all the spices. Cream the butter until soft and beat in ⅓ cup of the sugar until light and fluffy. Stir in the molasses and vanilla. Gradually add the flour, mixing it well. Refrigerate the dough for an hour or so until it is firm.

Preheat oven to 375°F. Adjust the racks to divide the oven into thirds. Butter 2 baking sheets, or line them with foil. Using a rounded teaspoon as a measure, roll bits of dough

between your hands to form balls 1 inch in diameter, about the size of a large cherry. Roll the balls in the remaining sugar, flattening them slightly.

Place the balls about 1½ inches apart on the baking sheets. Bake for 12 to 16 minutes, until the cookies are crackled on top and dry. After 7 or 8 minutes, reverse the baking sheets from top to bottom and from front to back. Transfer to a rack to cool.

Chocolate Cinnamon Cookies

50 cookies

2 ounces unsweetened chocolate (2 squares)
6 ounces unsalted butter
1 cup granulated sugar
1 egg, lightly beaten

½ teaspoon vanilla extract
2 tablespoons milk
2 cups all-purpose flour
½ teaspoon ground cinnamon
¼ teaspoon salt

Preheat oven to 375°F. Adjust the racks, placing them one above the center and the other below the center. Melt the chocolate in a small pot or bowl over simmering water; set aside. Cream the butter until soft, then beat in the sugar until the mixture is smooth and light. Add the egg, vanilla, melted chocolate and milk and beat well. Sift the flour before measuring and resift it with the cinnamon. Stir in the salt. Stir the flour into the mixture until thoroughly combined.

Drop by teaspoons about 2 inches apart on ungreased baking sheets. These can also be formed by rolling teaspoons of the dough between your hands to make a ball. Place these on the baking sheet, leaving 2 inches between them. Dip a fork into cold water and use the back of the tines to flatten out the balls.

Bake for about 10 minutes, until they are crisp. Halfway through the baking time, reverse the baking sheets from top to bottom and from front to back. Transfer them to a rack to cool.

Chocolate Chips

45 cookies

1 cup plus 2 tablespoons sifted all-purpose flour	6 tablespoons firmly packed dark brown sugar
½ teaspoon baking soda	1 egg, lightly beaten
½ teaspoon salt	1 teaspoon vanilla extract
4 ounces unsalted butter	6 ounces semisweet chocolate bits (1 cup)
6 tablespoons granulated sugar	

Preheat oven to 375°F. Adjust the racks to divide the oven into thirds. Lightly butter 2 baking sheets, or line them with foil. Sift the flour before measuring and resift it with the baking soda and salt. Cream the butter with the 2 sugars until smooth and light. Beat in the egg and vanilla. When thoroughly blended, add the flour gradually until it is just incorporated. Fold in the chocolate bits.

Using a spoon and a rubber spatula or 2 spoons, drop the dough by lightly rounded teaspoons about 1½ inches apart onto greased or foil-lined baking sheets.

Bake them for 8 to 10 minutes. About halfway through the baking time, reverse the baking sheets from top to bottom and from front to back. Cookies are done when they spring back when gently pressed with a fingertip. Remove from baking sheets and cool on a rack.

Brownies

16 squares

½ cup sifted all-purpose flour
¼ teaspoon salt
6 tablespoons unsalted butter
1 cup granulated sugar
2 eggs
½ teaspoon vanilla extract

2 ounces unsweetened chocolate (2 squares), melted and cooled slightly
1 cup walnut or pecan halves or large pieces

Preheat oven to 325°F. Place a rack on the middle level. Butter an 8-inch-square pan, line it with wax paper, and butter and flour the paper; shake off the excess flour.

Sift the flour before measuring and resift it with the salt. (See Note.) Cream the butter and beat in the sugar. Add the eggs, one at a time, beating after each addition, and beat in the melted chocolate and the vanilla. Add the sifted dry ingredients and beat until just mixed. Fold in the nuts and turn mixture into the prepared pan.

Bake for 25 to 30 minutes. Brownies should be moist; they are done when a toothpick inserted in the center comes out barely clean. Allow cake to cool in the pan for about 30 minutes. Place a rack or cookie sheet over the pan and invert it. Remove the pan and the wax paper, cover with another rack or cookie sheet, and invert again. Slide onto a cutting board. With a thin sharp knife, cut into 2-inch squares or 1 × 2-inch bars.

Note: For a less dense brownie, add ½ teaspoon baking powder to the sifted flour.

Blondies

16 squares

6 tablespoons unsalted butter
¾ cup firmly packed dark brown sugar
1 egg, beaten

1 teaspoon vanilla extract
¾ cup sifted all-purpose flour
1 teaspoon baking powder
¼ teaspoon salt
¾ cup coarsely chopped nuts

Preheat oven to 350°F. Place the rack on the middle level. Butter an 8-inch-square baking pan, line it with wax paper, and butter the paper. Cream the butter until soft. Add the brown sugar, beating until the mixture is fluffy. Add the egg and the vanilla and beat well. Sift the flour before measuring, then sift again with the baking powder and salt, and add it to the batter. Fold in the nuts and scrape the batter into the prepared baking pan.

Bake for about 30 minutes, or until a toothpick inserted in the center comes out just barely clean. The blondies should be moist in the middle. Allow them to cool completely in the pan, about 30 minutes.

Place a rack or baking sheet over the pan and invert it. Remove the pan and the wax paper. Cover with another rack and invert again so that the cake is right side up. Transfer it to a cutting board. With a thin sharp knife cut into long strips, then crosswise into squares.

Mocha Walnut Cookies

36 cookies

2 cups all-purpose flour
1½ teaspoons baking powder
½ teaspoon salt
4 ounces unsalted butter
1⅓ cups granulated sugar
2 large eggs, lightly beaten

1 teaspoon vanilla extract
⅓ cup prepared strong coffee
2 ounces (2 squares) unsweetened chocolate
½ cup chopped walnuts

Sift the flour before measuring and resift it with the baking powder and salt. Cream the butter with the sugar until light and fluffy. Add the beaten eggs and vanilla and mix well. Heat the coffee and melt the chocolate in the coffee. Add the melted chocolate and coffee to the batter, then the flour. Mix well and fold in the walnuts. Chill the dough for about 2 hours.

Preheat oven to 350°F. Adjust the racks, placing them one above the center and one below. Butter 2 baking sheets. Remove the dough from the refrigerator. With your hands, form it into balls about 1 inch in diameter. Place the balls 2 to 3 inches apart on the prepared baking sheets.

Bake for 12 to 15 minutes. After 7 or 8 minutes, reverse the baking sheets from top to bottom and from front to back. Cookies will be quite soft, so let them cool on the sheets for about 5 minutes before transferring them to a rack.

Marmalade Bars

32 bars

1¼ cups boiling water
1 cup rolled oats, preferably old-fashioned
1½ cups sifted all-purpose flour
1 teaspoon baking soda
½ teaspoon salt
½ teaspoon ground cinnamon
¼ teaspoon grated nutmeg
⅛ teaspoon ground cloves
4 ounces unsalted butter

1 cup granulated sugar, or ½ cup firmly packed dark brown sugar and ½ cup granulated sugar
1 teaspoon vanilla extract
2 eggs
6 tablespoons dark orange marmalade
confectioners' sugar (optional)

Pour the boiling water over the oats. Set them aside, covered, for 20 minutes.

Preheat oven to 350°F. Place a rack on the middle level. Butter and flour an 8-inch-square pan, shaking out the excess flour. Sift the flour before measuring and resift it with the baking soda, salt and all the spices. In a large bowl cream the butter until soft, and beat in the sugar (or sugars) until light and fluffy. Beat in the vanilla and add the eggs, one at a time, beating after each addition. Stir in the oats. Gradually add the sifted dry ingredients, mixing just until incorporated.

Spread half of the mixture in the prepared pan. Spread evenly with the marmalade and top with the remaining half of the batter.

Bake for about 40 minutes, until the top springs back when gently pressed and the edges of the cake have pulled away from the pan. Dust with confectioners' sugar, if you like, while the cake is still warm. Let cake cool in the pan before cutting into bars.

Variation: Substitute ginger marmalade, apricot preserves or raspberry preserves for the orange marmalade.

Part Five

WELCOMING THE SPRING

The end of winter is cause for celebration. As the days lengthen, spirits lighten, and a springtime dinner party is the perfect opportunity for the host and hostess to take advantage of this phenomenon.

To the cook, the marketplace brings signs of spring that are at least as welcome as the first robins and daffodils. For most of America this means asparagus and strawberries, eastern seacoast shad and western salmon and Dungeness crab. But there is one springtime delicacy much favored in Europe that is just beginning to be appreciated in this country. The French dote on sorrel *(oseille),* a sour potherb with which they make soup and a classic sauce for salmon and shad. Eastern European Jews make their celebrated soup, *schav,* with sorrel, beaten egg and a pinch of sugar. It is a taste worth cultivating.

Your springtime dinner party can be decorated with daffodils, tulips, primroses, narcissus, pots of fresh herbs, or whatever your garden or florist can provide. One hostess, a venerable southern lady, arranges the pale green curled leaves of young rhubarb in silver pots down the center of her table. Apple blossoms make showy arrangements and grape hyacinths could be interspersed with mounds of baby artichokes for a memorable centerpiece.

What better way to begin your rite of spring than with a steaming creamy soup of sorrel or asparagus, delicately thickened with egg yolk and cream? The soup can be made several days in advance, with the cream and yolk enrichment added at the last minute. Poached salmon is our choice for the main course, but if salmon is not available in your area, boned shad or striped bass will make an excellent substitute. A plain hollandaise sauce is the traditional accompaniment, but you may want to consider a mousseline, a hollandaise mixed with whipped cream. Our more delicate mousseline, which has been lightened with beaten egg whites and flavored with snipped chives, is another delicious alternative. This mousseline is also delicious accompanying asparagus as a first course, and serves as an admirable dipping sauce for globe artichokes. It should be made not more than 2 hours before serving time and kept unrefrigerated.

A handful of fresh dill folded into a hollandaise is another springtime variation on the traditional sauce.

Cucumbers, blanched briefly in salted water and tossed in hot butter, garnished with dill, accompany the salmon. Your starch can be a crusty loaf of French bread, the perfect sponge for those last delectable bits of sauce.

A luscious strawberry "shortcake" made with old-fashioned poundcake and strawberries flavored with Jamaican rum is the grand finale, accompanied by whipped cream, which you may want to serve plain, with powdered sugar and a dash of liqueur, or mixed with sour cream for a *crème fraîche.* (The proportions are 2 cups heavy sweet cream to 1 cup sour cream.) Little thimbles of strawberry liqueur served straight from the freezer may provide an interesting accompaniment to the dessert. Other fruit liqueurs to complement the strawberries would be blackberry or raspberry *eau-de-vie,* or Kirschwasser, the famous German cherry brandy from the Black Forest.

SPRING DINNER FOR SIX

Cream of Asparagus Soup
or
Cream of Sorrel Soup

Poached Salmon with Hollandaise

Sautéed Cucumbers with Dill

French Bread

Jamaican Fantasy Strawberry Shortcake

Wine Suggestion: Pinot Chardonnay

Chardonnays

The axiom "white wine with fish, red wine with meat" has been somewhat supplanted lately by its corollary "your own taste should be your guide." While it is true, of course, that personal taste should be the final arbiter, there is a reason why fish dishes are better when combined with a more subtle, delicate white wine rather than a hearty Burgundy or Cabernet Sauvignon. The flavors of the fish dishes are enhanced, not overpowered and, while there are light red wines such as a Beaujolais or rosé that are lovely, any well-chilled bottle of white Burgundy is the most complementary.

The magnificent Premier Cru estates of Meursault and Montrachet in France produce some of the finest white Burgundies available. Such classics as a Puligny Montrachet or a Meursault are magnificent dry white wines that your guests can enjoy before the meal or with the salmon. These wines tend to be more expensive than many other white wines such as a Vouvray or a Chablis, but their taste and complexity can make any meal a special occasion.

These wines are made from the Chardonnay grape, a versatile beauty that flourishes particularly well in the United States. While the adaptable Chardonnay has produced superior wines in the colder climes of the Eastern United States and Oregon and Washington, it is in California's Napa Valley that the classic Chardonnays are found. The Bargetto family produces one of the best wines available; also delicious are the Chardonnays produced by the wineries of Far Niente, Calistoga, Beringer and Pedroncelli, and several dozen more.

MARKET LIST

Meat and Fish

6-pound salmon

Fruit and Vegetables

8 ounces sorrel, or 24 asparagus stalks
carrot
leek
parsley
1 bunch of green onions (scallions)

1 small head of radicchio
5 cucumbers, about 3 pounds
fresh dill
lemons
2 pints strawberries

Staples

butter
chicken stock
eggs
cornstarch
heavy cream
thyme
white pepper

granulated sugar
flour
salt
vanilla extract
almond extract
dark Jamaican rum
confectioners' sugar

Cream of Asparagus Soup

This soup can be made 3 days ahead, up to the final enrichment with egg yolk and cream. Omit cornstarch for a thinner soup.

6 portions

24	asparagus stalks	2	teaspoons cornstarch
4	tablespoons butter, melted	2	cups heavy cream
1	quart rich chicken stock	2	egg yolks

Wash and scale asparagus. Steam the stalks until just crunchy. Cut off and reserve the tips. Cut the rest of the stalks into 1-inch pieces and sauté in the butter in a nonaluminum pan for 3 minutes. Add stock, bring to a boil, lower heat, and simmer for 15 minutes. Cool. Put the soup, in batches, in a blender or food processor and purée it. Combine the batches and return the soup to the saucepan. Dissolve cornstarch in a few drops of water, then stir it into the cream. Combine egg yolks with cream and mix thoroughly. Reheat the soup and pour in the cream mixture. Cook over gentle heat, do not let it boil, but simmer for 5 minutes. Stir in the reserved asparagus tips and serve at once.

Cream of Sorrel Soup

6 portions

8	ounces sorrel leaves	2	cups heavy cream
4	tablespoons butter, melted	2	egg yolks
1	quart rich chicken stock		salt and pepper
1	tablespoon cornstarch		

Strip sorrel leaves from their stems. Wash and dry leaves. Sauté sorrel in the melted butter in a nonaluminum pan; this is called "melting" the sorrel. Pour in the chicken stock and bring to a boil. Lower heat and simmer for 10 minutes. Cool. Put the soup, in batches, in a blender or food processor, and purée it; combine the batches and force the purée through a sieve, pressing out the sorrel purée. Dissolve the cornstarch in a few drops of water, then stir it into the cream. Combine egg yolks with the cream and mix thoroughly. Pour the mixture into the strained soup and heat it gently, taking care not to let it boil. Season to taste. Serve piping hot.

Poached Salmon

*If you have a fish poacher or a pan that can be adapted to
use for the purpose, poach the salmon in court bouillon.
If you lack a fish poacher, steam the salmon in foil;
directions follow.*

6 to 8 portions

1 salmon, 6 pounds	1 bunch of watercress

White-Wine Court Bouillon

1 carrot	6 parsley sprigs
1 leek	1 quart water
¼ teaspoon dried thyme	2 cups white wine

Have the salmon scaled and whole-dressed; head, tail and
fins are left intact. Make the court bouillon: Scrub and chop
carrot and leek and put in a fish poacher with thyme, parsley,
water and wine. Bring the bouillon to a boil, reduce to a
simmer, cover, and cook for 30 minutes. Let the court bouillon cool. Place fish on a rack and lower the rack into the
poacher. Cover the pan and simmer for about 30 minutes, or
for 10 minutes per inch, measured at the thickest point. Let
the fish cool in the liquid for 20 minutes.

Lift the fish from the poacher and place it on a thick
layer of cloth. Remove the skin, and the dark layer of flesh on
top and along the backbone. Garnish the fish with green
strips of scallions and place on a bed of radicchio. Serve
warm or at room temperature.

Foil-Steamed Salmon

6 to 8 portions

1 salmon, 6 pounds, whole-dressed	4 ounces butter, melted
	½ cup white wine

Place a large sheet of heavy-duty aluminum foil on a baking
sheet and drizzle the foil with 2 tablespoons of the melted
butter. Rub the salmon with more of the butter and place it on
the foil. Pour the rest of the butter and the wine over the fish.

Fold up the foil to enclose the fish and wrap it securely. Set
the baking sheet in a preheated 450°F oven and let it steam
for 10 minutes per pound. When the fish is cool, prepare it for
serving in the same fashion as the poached salmon.

Sautéed Cucumbers with Dill

6 portions

5 medium-size cucumbers,
about 3 pounds
4 tablespoons butter, melted

4 tablespoons snipped fresh
dill
salt and pepper

Peel cucumbers, halve them, and remove the seeds. Cut cucumbers into ½-inch slices and drop into a large saucepan of boiling water. Parboil for 1 minute; drain. Toss cucumbers in the melted butter and sprinkle with the dill and salt and pepper to taste. Serve piping hot.

Hollandaise Sauce

Double recipe (See Index)

Mousseline Sauce

3 cups hollandaise sauce

6 tablespoons heavy cream

Whip 6 tablespoons heavy cream to the mousse stage (soft mounds, not stiff), and fold into 3 cups hollandaise sauce.

Light Mousseline Sauce with Chives

3 cups hollandaise sauce
4 egg whites

¼ cup snipped fresh chives

Beat 4 egg whites stiff; snip enough fresh chives to make ¼ cup. Fold egg whites and chives into 3 cups hollandaise sauce.

Jamaican Fantasy Strawberry "Shortcake"

This pound cake can be made a week in advance. When it is cool, keep it tightly covered. Macerate the strawberries for 2 to 4 hours before you plan to serve the dessert. Assemble the dessert just before serving.

6 portions

Pound Cake

8	ounces butter		½	teaspoon salt
1⅔	cup sugar		1	teaspoon vanilla extract
5	eggs, separated		1	teaspoon almond extract
2	cups flour, sifted			

Strawberry Topping

4	cups sliced strawberries		½	cup dark Jamaican rum
½	cup sugar			

Jamaican Whipped Cream

2	cups heavy cream		¼	cup dark Jamaican rum
4	tablespoons confectioners' sugar			

Make the cake: Cream the butter and sugar together. Stir in eggs and flavorings. Gradually add the flour and salt. When the batter is well mixed, pour it into a well-buttered and floured loaf pan, 9 × 5 × 3 inches. Bake in a preheated 325°F oven for 1 hour and 15 minutes, or until a cake tester inserted in the center comes out clean.

Mix strawberries with ½ cup sugar and ½ cup rum and let them macerate in the refrigerator for 2 hours. Whip the cream with the confectioners' sugar and ¼ cup rum until it forms stiff peaks.

To serve, place a slice of pound cake on a serving plate and spoon ½ cup of the strawberry mixture over it. Top with the rum-flavored whipped cream.

INDEX